Letters from the Dead

Fredonia Books
Amsterdam, The Netherlands

Letterts from the Dead:
Last Letters from Soviet Men and Women who
Died Fighting the Nazis (1941-1945)

Translated from the Russian by
Jim Riordan

ISBN: 1-4101-0238-6

Reprinted from the 1965 edition

Fredonia Books
Amsterdam, The Netherlands
http://www.fredoniabooks.com

LETTERS FROM THE DEAD

From these pages speak out the dead, those who died fighting the nazi invaders between 1941 and 1945. This is a collection of their letters and documents written in the last minutes of their lives – in a Gestapo cell, a concentration camp or in the heat of battle. Here is a passionate call for triumph over fascism and world reaction, an appeal to those who survived to carry on the fight for mankind's future happiness, for eternal peace among all men.

These words of farewell written by Soviet partisans, underground fighters, soldiers, girls and boys driven into captivity, give an exceptionally penetrating insight into the Soviet character—the moral integrity, faith in victory, hatred for the foe and fervent patriotism.

CONTENTS

4

TO THOSE WHO SURVIVED

Those heroic and tragic war years 1941-45 are gradually fading into the past. But the further they get from us and the more the war wounds heal, the better perspective we have on the titanic efforts of their victims.

Mankind will never forget them, those who gave their lives to save others from slavery, to shield human civilisation and bring long-awaited peace.

Dear reader, you have before you a collection of documents left by Soviet patriots who died for the liberation and happiness of their country. Most of these letters, testaments, diaries and notes were written just a few days, hours or even minutes before death in a nazi prison cell, on the battlefield or in the rear.

These deeply-moving and awe-inspiring last lines cannot but induce a feeling of pride and admiration for these brave men and women. They spared no effort, not even their lives to safeguard their country's independence, to smash fascism and the "New Order" in Europe.

During the four years of their struggle against a formidable and ruthless enemy, the Soviet people battled with the Germans on a front stretching from the Arctic Ocean to the Black Sea.

The war demanded countless sacrifices. The nazis were sweeping aside all life and freedom that lay in their path, were despoiling and trampling underfoot the dearest and most precious human values. Hitler's men overran Europe to bleed white Soviet people and make them subservient to the German bankers and industrial magnates.

Once in the hands of their executioners, many men and women courageously withstood all trials and torments, preferring to die by enemy bullet rather than betray a comrade. Through the innumerable acts of heroism we can feel the unbroken spirit, the intrepid faith in victory over fascism, the supremacy of communist over fascist ideas.

At first losses were many and defeats common. In defence Soviet troops stood firm, then switched to the offensive driving the nazis from the country and bringing freedom to Europe and liberation from the nazi terror. No matter where the combat, Soviet patriots fought to the bitter end. And they won.

On the field of battle, in a prison cell or in a partisan dugout, many of them jotted down their innermost thoughts and noble feelings. Some used their old letters, some a scrap of paper, others their Party or Y.C.L. card, their handkerchiefs or head-scarfs to write to their near and dear ones, to their comrades-in-arms of their faith in victory and readiness to lay down their lives for a happy future.

From these pages speak the fearless warriors who were the first to bar the way to the nazi forces. On the Western frontier, close to the Ukrainian village of Paripsa, some 136 border-guards bore the brunt of a first assault. For an hour and a half they held at bay 16 tanks advancing along the Zhitomir-Kiev highway. Junior Lieutenant Sinokop took a scrap of paper and wrote what was to become a solemn pledge to all who fell in battle: "I'm going to die for my country. The enemy won't take me alive."

We do not know the names of the other border-guards. What we do know is that they were all staunch heroes.

Then come the brief notes from the Brest Fortress defenders:

"There were five of us: Sedov, I. Grutov, Bogolyub, Mikhailov, V. Selivanov. We beat back the first attack on 22.VI.41 at 3.15. We shall die but not retreat!"

"We'll die but won't desert the fortress."

"I am dying but won't surrender! Farewell, my country. 20/VII-41."

Many hundred miles separate Brest from Moscow, but this is where the main nazi drive on Moscow started. And it was here that a few hundred valiant men made a last ditch stand in their fortress and brought a German division to a halt for a whole month. As they shot their last rounds, the defenders, shedding their blood but never their courage, wrote their final words on the fortress walls, words of tenderness to their families, their country and their Party. So it was everywhere.

Everywhere sons and daughters gave their last breath to save their homeland from the nazi marauders.

As they faced their executioners the authors of these notes met their death with heads raised high.

"... Today, tomorrow—I don't know when—they are going to shoot me because I cannot go against my conscience, because I am a Komsomol girl. I'm not afraid to die and I shall die calmly," wrote Yelena Ubiivovk, one of the members of a big underground organisation in Poltava. All she regretted was that she had been able to do so little in her 20 years.

Another letter is by young Communist Ivan Kozlov, a key member of the Minsk underground caught by the Germans. He spent two months in prison under constant torture and interrogation. But nothing could break his will. Just before his execution he wrote to his comrades: "No tears. No despair. Our blood won't be shed in vain.

"Have courage, be brave, don't be afraid and never despair.

"I would give anything to live and get revenge on these savages! That you must do. If only I were able.... You can bet your life I would have slaughtered these dirty swine.... Yet only a couple of years ago I was too scared even to carve a little chicken...."

Many people volunteered to remain behind the lines and eagerly carried out the responsible work they were given.

With heavy heart, Leonid Silin bade farewell to his home. Like many other patriots he volunteered for the front. War is cruel. In his last note to his wife and children he wrote: "I want to hug and kiss you for the last time. Today I am to be shot by order of the German Command.... I die for my country, for our Party, for all Russians, Ukrainians, Byelorussians and all other people in the land, and for you. Love our country like I loved her, fight for her like I have and, if need be, die for her like me!"

Among the heroes who fought until their last breath on the approaches to Moscow were soldiers under the command of Alexander Vinogradov. They barred the way to the swastika'd tanks. "Three of us left: Kolya, Volodya and I, Alexander.... There goes another—Volodya from Moscow. The tanks keep coming at us. Only two of us now. But we shall hold out as long as we can.... Now there's only me, wounded in the head and arm. But we've knocked out more tanks. That makes 23 of them."

Here is a strength of character that will never die: three, two, one, mortally wounded, and 23 tanks are put out of action. There must have been many heroes like Alexander Vinogradov and his comrades or the famous 28 Panfilov men who fought to the last man.

The poet-martyr and hero Musa Jalil, executed in a Berlin prison, wrote this spirited call to battle:

> Today the last of my songs I sing:
> The axe hangs over my head.
> It was songs that taught me freedom to prize,
> Now they bid me to die like a fighter,
> My life was a love-song that soared to the skies;
> Let my death be the battle-song of a fighter.

Some of Jalil's poems were preserved and returned to the Soviet Union by a member of the Belgian Resistance Movement who had shared a cell with the poet. In this and many other ways anti-fascists from all over Europe joined hands and forged an unshakable friendship. Languages of many nations are inscribed on the walls of the "Death Fortress" set up by the Germans just outside Kaunas. "Keep up your spirits even in this cess-pit. Victory is ours! Workers of the world, unite!"—words in Russian, Rumanian, French and English, scrawled on the solitary-cell wall in the Tiraspol Gestapo prison.

By their bravery and sheer guts, Soviet heroes became an inspiration to anti-fascist fighters the world over.

As you read these letters you cannot help appreciating the lofty ideals and communist principles which have always motivated the actions of the best people of the Soviet land. They have faith in the coming of a society without wars or plunder, a love for communism and their homeland, a desire for comradeship and friendship among all nations.

The thoughts of the Soviet people in prison cells often turned to the past, weighing up the good and the bad and passing judgement on themselves. These are quite ordinary men and women and when the time came for heroism they did not flinch. They gave all they could for victory and did it as a matter of course. And the knowledge that they were laying down their lives for the people lightened their cruel fate. Almost everyone of the letters mentions this. These anti-fascist warriors used the slightest opportunity to inform the folks at home, their comrades and countrymen that Hitler's hangmen had not broken their will. They called out to those alive to mercilessly crush their murderers.

Riga underground hero Imant Sudmalis and Donetsk Komsomol and underground leader Savva Matekin both bear witness to this undying faith and iron will.

"When I look back over the days gone by, I have nothing to reproach myself for," wrote Imant Sudmalis in a Gestapo dungeon before he was hanged. "I acted like a man and a fighter in those fateful days."

While waiting to be shot, Savva Matekin shared his last thoughts with his wife: "What can a man do when he is in the death cell? All the same they're scared of me. Tell that to our people. . . ."

At the time of the country's most harrowing tribulations, thousands of people became giants among men and appeared to the world as titans moulded from head to foot of pure steel.

"The horrors of war must never return! Peace will triumph and life will prosper again!" That was the wish of these legendary heroes. We shall never forget them. And we must ensure their last wish is observed.

Every letter has its own story. Before they arrived in this collection most of them travelled a hard and often perilous journey, through many hands, along the rutted roads of war. Keeping them often entailed mortal danger for those behind the lines. They preserved them as their most precious possession. Many similar letters were consumed in the flames of war and, no doubt, more than a few still lie undiscovered.

These letters, notes, inscriptions on walls, diary excerpts, etc., are presented in chronological order and divided into sections where they happen to be connected by one particular place or author, in which case they are arranged according to the date of the last letter.

Each letter has a short note on its author and the conditions under which it was written.

You may die, but in the song
of the brave and the strong in
heart, you will forever be a
living example, a proud appeal
for liberty and reason.

Maxim Gorky

INSCRIPTIONS
ON THE WALLS OF THE BREST FORTRESS

June 22-July 20, 1941

There were five of us: Sedov, I. Grutov, Bogolyub, Mikhailov, V. Selivanov. We fought the first attack on 22.VI.1941 at 3.15. We shall die but not retreat!

We'll die but won't desert the fortress.

I am dying but won't surrender! Farewell, my country. 20/VII–41.

The defence of the Brest Fortress* between June and July 1941 has gone down in history as an immortal act of valour by Soviet soldiers who, though fighting against countless odds, held off many enemy assaults and never surrendered.

Against the fortress manned by only a small garrison, the nazi High Command used its 45th Infantry Division which included nine light and three heavy artillery batteries and was reinforced by the 27th Artillery Regiment, plus nine howitzers and heavy mortars.

Despite the advantage gained by their surprise attack the Germans failed to take the fortress by storm. Appreciating the gravity of the situation, the fortress officers rapidly rearranged command over the defence operations. On the third day of battle, June 24, 1941, Order No. 1 was issued to the garrison. It stated that the situation demanded a unified command and co-ordinated action against the enemy, that all the remaining forces were to be combined into a single group under the command of Captain Ivan Zubachov, with Regimental Commissar Yefim Fomin as his political assistant.

---

* For the whole amazing story of the Fortress defenders, see *Heroes of Brest Fortress*, S. Smirnov, Progress Publishers, Moscow.

An inscription on the wall of the Brest Fortress

The fortress defenders were still beating off enemy attacks when on June 27 German tanks entered Minsk, the Byelorussian capital. When, on June 16, practically a whole month after the outbreak of war, the ancient Russian town of Smolensk fell, the Brest Fortress still stood as a redoubtable bastion deep in the rear of Hitler's armies and, cut off from the rest of the world (their wireless was put out of action in the first few days), they still held out using grenades, rifles and machine-guns to beat back the frantic enemy. There was no water, food supplies were running out, but the fortress defenders gave no thought to surrendering.

When the plan to take the fortress by infantry attacks failed, the 12th German Corps commanders concentrated artillery fire from the neighbouring 31st and 34th divisions on the fortress. Mass bombing raids continued. But the men still thwarted the Germans. And in answer to the enemy's offer to them to surrender, a strip of cloth was hung from one of the fortress walls. On it were the words in blood: "We shall all die for our country, but we won't surrender!"

Even the nazis, who had conquered almost all Europe, were struck by the firmness and courage of the Soviet men and women in the fortress. Among the captured staff papers of the 45th German Infantry Division a battle report was discovered which contained the following acknowledgement:

"Overwhelming attacks on a fortress defended by a courageous garrison cost a lot of blood. This simple truth has been proved yet again in the capture of the Brest Fortress. The Russians in Brest-Litovsk fought with exceptional stubbornness and determination, they displayed superb infantry training and a splendid will to resist."

An inscription on the barrack wall of the Brest Fortress

Most of the valiant defenders of the Brest Fortress met their death, including the commanding officers. Yefim Fomin, seriously wounded, was captured by the Germans and shot. Captain Zubachov died in a German concentration camp.

In the tiny group of defenders who did come out alive was Brest hero Major Pyotr Gavrilov, former CO of the 44th Infantry Regiment. It was Gavrilov, more dead than alive, who led the last battle. Wounded and shell-shocked, he fell into nazi hands. German officers respectfully regarded him as a man of uncommon persistence and faith in victory.

Excavations among the ruins of the fortress unearthed the remains of soldiers, banners, guns and personal papers. Many inscriptions made by the heroic defenders have been found on the stone arches, walls and stairs.

NOTE
FROM JUNIOR LIEUTENANT
NIKOLAI SINOKOP

22 June 1941

Ass. Com. Border-Post, Junior Lieutenant Nikolai Sinokop. Bobrik village, Romensk District, Sumy Region.

I'll die for my country. The enemy won't take me alive.

22.6.41.

Nikolai Sinokop was born into a peasant's family on June 5, 1918, in the village of Bobrik in Sumy Region. In 1938, he was called up to serve in the Red Army. Two years later he was commissioned to Junior Lieutenant and appointed assistant commander of a border-post on the western frontier of the Soviet Union.

At the outbreak of war, the border-guards were the first to bear the brunt of the nazi attack. Many fierce battles took place between the men guarding the frontier and the leading German units. The enemy had immense advantage and was supported by tanks and artillery. The dauntless border-guards had nothing to repulse the assault with but machine- and submachine-guns and rifles. Despite the heavy odds the guards put up staunch resistance to the tanks.

Like thousands of his frontier comrades, Komsomol member Nikolai Sinokop found himself in the heat of the battle in the very first hours of the war. It was then that he vowed to fight to the last breath and not let the enemy through. He took off his medallion* and wrote the words of his pledge on the same paper as his name and place of birth.

---

* Identity cylinder, a plastic cylinder used in the Soviet Army as an identification disc.

After stubborn, bloody and grossly unequal pitched battles with the enemy, the surviving border-guards had to retreat eastwards. Combining in a foot-column of about two hundred men they made their way along the Zhitomir-Kiev highway.

On July 13, 1941, somewhere between 10 and 11 a.m., the column, which had left the town of Skvir and was heading for the village of Popelnya, was overtaken by 16 nazi tanks. On the outskirts of Paripsa (some 3 miles from Popelnya) the guards decided to engage the enemy. At a signal from their commanding officer the soldiers quickly fanned out over the village vegetable plots and dug in. One group under Jun. Lt. Sinokop lay in wait on a small hill to the north-west of the village. Without any anti-tank weapons, the border-guards fearlessly battled it out on the open ground with the black-swastika'd tanks for an hour and a half. But the odds were too great.

After the battle, peasants from neighbouring villages picked up among the deserted and burning tanks and buried 136 dead border-guards. Among the papers discovered on the dead men was this note folded inside Jun. Lt. Sinokop's identification cylinder.

TESTAMENT
BY BINA LURJE, A PRIVATE OF THE 1ST LATVIAN
VOLUNTEER REGIMENT

August 26-28, 1941

TESTAMENT

Please convey this to my mother Mrs. Lurje, an evacuee from Latvia, now living in Kirov.

I die for my country, for communism. It's two months now since this fierce battle with the enemy began. For me the last stage of the fight has now come—the battle for Tallinn. There can be no retreat.

It's hard to die at 24, but for such a worthy cause, when millions of lives are held in the balance of history, I, too, give my life, knowing that future generations and you who remain among the living, will honour and remember us as the world's liberators from a horrible plague. What more is there to write?

Mum,

Don't take it too badly.

I'm not the first nor the last to give my life for communism, for my country.

Long live the U.S.S.R. and victory over the enemy!

Y.C.L. member of the Latvian
Regiment
Bina Lurje

The 1st Latvian Volunteer Infantry Regiment, formed in the very first days of the war and attached to the 8th Army took part in those furious defensive battles against the German assault on Latvia and Estonia in the summer of 1941.

In August 1941, together with other Army and Navy units, the regiment defended Tallinn, the capital of Soviet Estonia.

Bina Lurje served in this regiment. Back in bourgeois Latvia he had been a fighter for his people's liberation. The Ulmanis court had sentenced him to penal servitude for his communist activities. But that did not crush the young patriot's will. When the Soviets set him free in 1940 he gave himself fully to his work, even though he was a sick man.

As soon as war broke out, Bina Lurje joined the volunteers. He defended Tallinn to his last round, to his last drop of blood, and was killed in the street fighting. The memory of this brave and dedicated man left a deep trace on the minds of his comrades.

After his death, his comrades-in-arms discovered in his pocket this testament placed in his Y.C.L. card.

EXTRACTS FROM PROF. LEONID KULIK'S
LETTERS TO HIS WIFE

October 21-28, 1941

October 21, 1941. District village of Vskhody,*
Smolensk Region

> *Autumn is waning; the rooks have departed;*
> *The forest stands naked, the fields lie deserted.*

Bleak, windy and rainy. The snow has melted, the last leaves
on the trees rustle and float through the air one by one. There
isn't a soul about in the village, people are hiding in the few
decent houses left. All that lives is the highway teeming with
German vehicles of all shapes and sizes. And sometimes there
are long columns of prisoners.

Grief has cast her shadow over our country.

What am I? Who am I?

First of all I am wounded. My leg wound is improving,
but slowly, since I'm on the go from morning to night as I
am, in the second place, a medical instructor. To put it plainly,
I'm medical orderly in an infirmary for the Soviet wounded in
the village of Vskhody.

First I was on the dressings and operations and also a
kind of general help. Now they have put me in charge of the
general anaesthetic during operations and attached me to the
children's ward. It has six patients: Manya, Nina, Panya (all
3-5 years old), Vanya (12), Dusya and Polya (17).

---

* In this village the Germans set up a "hospital" and left Soviet
wounded soldiers to die there.

... Dead of night. A thick, putrid stench of festering wounds.... The close, oppressive, sticky air is filled with groans, animal-like wailing, wild shrieks.... It's unbearably stuffy. In the dim light from the splinter painfully glistens the blue eye (the other is smashed) of a boy, a good boy, his stomach ripped open by a shell splinter.

Leonid Kulik was born in 1883. After leaving school he studied at Kazan University. But he was not to finish his studies. He was in charge of an organisation of the Russian Social-Democratic Labour Party. On instructions from the Bolshevik centre he carried out a raid on a tsarist prison to liberate a condemned revolutionary. The bold plan paid off but Kulik himself was arrested and exiled to Orenburg Gubernia.

There he worked as a forester's assistant, which suited him well since he was a great nature lover. He collected minerals, studied plant life and geology and became an expert on mineralogy, ornithology and botany.

After the 1917 Revolution his work and knowledge were widely recognised and he became Scientific Secretary to the Meteorite Commission of the U.S.S.R. Academy of Sciences. He journeyed all over the country in search of meteorites.

He was particularly fascinated by the riddle of the Tunguska meteorite. He gave twenty years of his life to this problem, during which time he made countless expeditions to the place where the giant Tunguska meteorite had fallen. These were difficult journeys which entailed much danger and sacrifice, all willingly endured for the purpose of unravelling the secret.

When war broke out, Prof. Kulik was 60. But he joined the ranks of the people's volunteer detachments. Neither the Academy of Sciences nor the entreaties of his colleagues and wife could persuade him to remain in Moscow. He had made up his mind that his place was alongside the anti-fascist fighters.

And so, a hard life at the front began for the elderly scientist. Soviet troops were on the retreat. In the autumn of 1941, during a battle near Spass-Demensk on the Smolensk plain, a group of men including Leonid Kulik found themselves behind the lines. They decided to fight their way back. Soon they ran into an enemy patrol. In the ensuing skirmish the professor was hit in the leg and lost consciousness. When he came to, he gritted his teeth and began crawling eastwards. His leg wound was agonising and he was craving for water. Once again he fainted. This time he regained consciousness in a nazi prison camp. Interrogations began. The Germans soon realised they had a noted Soviet scientist in their hands.

They tried everything to break him down. But they failed. Kulik got in touch with the villagers and through them with the partisans. He organised an infirmary in the camp and sat many long nights at the bedside of the wounded doing his best to relieve their suffering.

The partisans devised a plan for rescuing the professor. But it did not come off. One hour before the appointed time, the Germans sent him off to Spass-Demensk where he was pitched into a typhus barracks.

Here, too, he did what he could to ease the suffering of the delirious patients. But, faint with hunger, the old scientist's organism was not equal to it, and on the third day he, too, went down with typhoid fever. For a long time he raved in a delirium, fighting battles, escaping from the camp, calling to his wife and daughter, shouting something to the partisans, cursing the enemy and persuading someone to go with him in search of the Tunguska meteorite. Death cut short the scientist's sufferings. On April 14, 1942, Prof. Leonid Kulik passed away.

LETTER
FROM GUNNER-SCOUT ARKADY POLUEKTOV

October 1941

Dear Sasha,

If I die, write to my old people that I died painlessly and calmly. I hate fascism, I hate the bloody, plundering and murdering fascist scum. And if I had a second life, I'd give it too. Tell them I'm happy to have fought in this great battle.

Farewell, don't forget me,

Arkady Poluektov

In October of 1941, Moscow was in mortal danger. Hitler's armies had pushed on into Mozhaisk, Maloyaroslavets and Naro-Fominsk, not far from the capital.

The Naro-Fominsk sector of the front was being defended by the 33rd Army commanded by Lieutenant-General Yefremov. The battle did not let up day or night. Side by side with the Red Army regular detachments fought the soldiers of the people's volunteer corps of the Kuibyshev and Frunze districts of Moscow. The soldiers daily performed miracles of valour and daring. Every soldier knew that Moscow lay behind him and that the enemy had to be stopped at all costs.

In order to spot the enemy's firing points, gunner-scout Arkady Poluektov was always trying to crawl as close as he could to enemy lines so that his comrades on the gun batteries could pinpoint their target. One bleak October day the brave scout was fire-spotting from his vantage point. Enemy tanks and guns blew up into the air together with their crews on his directions. But Arkady was to scout no more. He lay dead, struck by an enemy bullet.

His last letter was written to his friend Alexander Gorbulin.

LETTER
FROM SOVIET SAILORS DEFENDING
THE MOONZUND ISLANDS

Late October 1941

Comrade Sailors of the Red Navy,

We, Baltic Fleet sailors on Dago Island, in this critical hour, vow to our government and Party that we shall fight to the last man rather than surrender our island.

We shall show the whole world that Soviet sailors know how to die having done their duty to their country with honour.

Farewell, comrades.

Avenge our death. Destroy the fascist scum.

Centre. Dago Island, Takhkun Peninsula.

Signed on behalf of us all
Kurochkin, Orlov, Konkin

For two months a small garrison on the Moonzund archipelago in the enemy's rear defended the island of Soviet Estonia. The enemy had to divert considerable forces to deal with this handful of brave men who were killing so many enemy soldiers, sinking ships and shooting down planes.

The last battles took place on the Takhkun horn, the most northernly tip of Khiuma (Dago) Island. It had fortified positions manned by a small garrison of sailors. On October 12, 1941, the Germans began large-scale landings on the island. Some 30 launches headed for the western beaches, near Nurst. Southwards near Terkma, 15 landing craft with an infantry regiment on board were hovering off-shore. The landings were covered by artillery from Sarem Island, from an enemy

28

cruiser and four destroyers, and by terrific bombardment from the air. The Khiuma defenders opened up on the enemy landing boats. The shore batteries sank about two dozen craft and launches. But the nazis brought up more and more reinforcements. Under cover of darkness they managed to get a landing party ashore and began to advance.

Soldiers of the 33rd Engineers' Battalion manned the defences of the southern bank. The battalion's machine-gunners succeeded in pegging the enemy back. For several days fierce fighting went on all over the island. On October 17, the island garrison retreated to the last outpost of defence. It stretched from Tarest to the west, covering the Takhkun Peninsula.

The Baltic Fleet Command decided to evacuate the island garrison to Hankö Peninsula. But stormy weather stopped the ships from putting in at the island. Only on October 19 did the launches succeed in taking the Khiuma Island defenders off.

Under constant fire and bombardment, a group of sailors covered the evacuation. Before the last decisive battle the Takhkun defenders wrote their letter of farewell, pledging to defend their native soil until their last cartridge, until their last drop of blood. Having sealed the letter in a bottle, they hurled it into the sea. At the beginning of the winter of 1941 the bottle was picked up in the open sea by sailors aboard a Soviet patrol vessel.

LETTER
FROM POLITICAL INSTRUCTOR NIKOLAI GATALSKY
TO HIS FAMILY

Not later than November 13, 1941*

Volkhov

My dear wife Stanislava, little Valya and mum,

Please excuse my bad writing. I'm having to write on a scrap of paper perched on my knees. Hurrying to let you know I'm alive and about to go into battle.

Maybe this letter will be the last, my dear ones. Dear Stanislava, look after our daughter and care for my mother. If you don't get any more news from me, you'll know I gave my life honourably for you and our beloved country.

Best of luck—your husband and father.

Stassya, once again, look after our little girl.

Love to you all,
Kolya

Nikolai Gatalsky was a regular officer in the Soviet Army. On finishing a three-year course in a military-political school he was appointed to the 144th Division. When war broke out he was transferred to another unit fighting on the Leningrad Front. "The fascists will never set foot in the city of Lenin," he used to tell the men and always himself headed the counter-attacks.

The fighting was at its hottest around Leningrad. Gatalsky's detachment took up the defence of a hamlet called Morozovo. On the

* Nikolai Gatalsky was killed in battle on November 13, 1941.

morning of November 13, 1941, the nazis began a fierce assault. It seemed that just one more push and the remaining heroes would be wiped out. But at that moment, the political instructor raised himself to his full height. Behind him rose the others. With their last hand-grenades they tore into the enemy shouting "hurrah".

When the battle died down, there on the snow, surrounded by nazi corpses, lay the political instructor. His men buried him on the outskirts of the village. Three volleys rang out. Then, Nikolai Gatalsky's comrades again rushed into the fray.

NOTE AND LETTER
FROM PARTISAN VERA PORSHNEVA
TO HER MOTHER

November 29, 1941

Tomorrow I die, Mum.

You've lived fifty years, and I only twenty-four, I so much want to live. How little I've done. I want to live to kill these hateful fascists. They've tortured me, but I haven't told them a thing. I know my partisan comrades will avenge my death. They'll wipe out the invaders.

Don't cry, Mum. I'll die knowing that I've done all I can for victory. It's no sin to die for the people. Tell all the girls to join the partisans, be brave and kick these uninvited dogs out of the country.

Victory is not far off!

LETTER TO HER MOTHER

November 30, 1941

My dear Mummy,

I'm writing this letter just before I die. When you get it I shall no longer be alive. Dear Mum, you mustn't cry over me, and you mustn't grieve too much. I'm not afraid of death. . . . Mummy, you are all alone and I don't know how you will get on without me. I think Zoya will look after you alright. Anyway, my dear one, you must get along somehow. Mum, I envy you a little all the same; you've already lived fifty years, but I have to die at 24, and how much I want to live and see the future. Never mind, enough of dreaming. . . .

I'll end now, I can't write any more. My hands are trembling and my head won't work. I've been without food now

32

for two days and nights, but it's easier to die on an empty stomach. You know, Mum, it's such a pity to die.

Well, never mind. Farewell, my dearest mother. I'd love to see you all, you, Zoya, dear little Zhenya. If he grows up to be a man, tell him what his auntie was like. Well that's all. All my love to you all, and to you, Mummy.

Your daughter Vera.

When the enemy had taken the western districts of Kalinin Region, a wide-scale partisan movement started up.

Vera Porshneva was trained as a machine-gunner and posted to a partisan unit where she was praised as a fearless and daring fighter.

A little later, she was given instructions to take up work in German Commandatura, and get all the information she could. She became the best scout in the partisan unit. Vera was given away by a traitor and fell into nazi hands. This happened in the hamlet of Borisovka. For twelve days, the Gestapo interrogated the girl using all their usual methods.

All without success. Her torturers tried a new trick: they let her go. Vera made up her mind to hide and later get back to her unit, but she was closely followed and two days later she was again seized and thrown into a stone cellar in a barn.

Inhuman tortures began. They forced white-hot needles under her nails, burnt her breast, drove her half naked into the snow, gave her neither water nor food. And only greater and greater hatred welled up in her eyes, eyes which before the war everyone had said were always so kind.

Vera knew death was not far off, but she didn't complain. She was confident in victory over the nazis. All she grieved for was her mother. On a tiny piece of grey paper Vera wrote a few lines to her, which bear the pain in her heart, sober words of comfort and confidence in a quick victory. But she didn't manage to get this note through. Just before her death she wrote another little letter which she sewed in the fold of her coat.

Before they shot her the brutal Gestapo branded a five-cornered star on the young heroine's breast. Vera Porshneva died on December 21, 1941.

Vera Porshneva

NOTE
FROM NAVAL MACHINE-GUNNER
ALEXEI KALUZHNY

December 20, 1941

My dear country! Dear Russian land! I, a son and pupil of Leninist Y.C.L., have fought as my heart directed me, I killed those bastards as long as my heart beat in my chest. I am dying, but I know we shall win. The enemy won't get into Sevastopol.

Black Sea sailors! Destroy the fascist mad dogs. I have kept my sailor's vow.

Kaluzhny

By mid-November 1941, the nazi forces had taken all Crimea with the exception of Sevastopol. The defence of this famous naval town lasted more than eight months. The enemy bore tremendous losses in men and weapons. Many brave sailors and naval officers of the redoubtable Black Sea Fleet met their death during those heroic and tragic days.

Naval machine-gunner Alexei Kaluzhny fought together with his comrades-in-arms in pill-box No. 11 located at a crucial point near the village of Dalny. For three days and nights the bold sailors fought off fierce enemy attacks. Nazi planes constantly bombed the pill-box and it was heavily shelled. Petty Officer S. S. Rayenko, A. V. Kaluzhny, D. I. Pogorelov, T. Dolya, I. Chetvertakov and others swore not to budge an inch. Their supplies were running out, smoke was blinding and choking them. Many sailors lay wounded. On the third night, November 19, they received some reinforcements—M. N. Potapenko, K. I. Korol and P. Korzh, bringing with them ammunition, food and some water. Thanks to this help the brave sailors held out for another 24 hours. But the odds were too great. On December 20, when all that was left were three gravely wounded sailors, the nazis stormed the height and overran the pill-box.

A few days later Soviet troops again beat back the enemy. In what was left of the dug-out they found nine of the fallen heroes. In the gas-mask bag of the dead gunner Alexei Kaluzhny, they found a scrap of paper—the sailor's last letter addressed to his fellow countrymen.

VOW BY IVAN ANDROSOV

December 1941

I go into battle a Communist, and I pledge that I shall fight bravely, skilfully and worthily, not begrudging my blood and even my life to wipe out this nazi plague. All I ask is, after fascism is destroyed, if I am killed, to let my parents know that I died for Lenin's cause. The address is Tatiana Androsova, Noviki Village, Malevichesky Village Soviet, Zhlobinsky District, Gomel Region, Byelorussian S.S.R.

I pledge I shall not leave the battlefield even if I am wounded as long as I have strength.

Comradely greetings,

Communist soldier Ivan Androsov

In the dark days of October 1941, Hitler's hordes tried to overrun the old Russian gunsmith town of Tula.

For many days, the soldiers fought a persistent battle against overwhelming odds.

On December 4 and 5, the town was almost completely surrounded. All highways linking it up with Moscow and the nearest district centres were cut off. Only to the north-west of Tula there remained a narrow strip of land which the enemy forces had not managed to overrun.

In one of the fierce encounters with Guderian panzer, a brave young Communist of the 150th Regiment, Ivan Androsov, met his end. The steel monsters were bearing down on a tiny handful of gallant soldiers who met them with hand grenades and incendiary bottles. The first, then the second and third stopped dead and burst into flames. But more came on. And as they came, Ivan Androsov hurriedly jotted down the last words he was ever to write. Three sheets from his notebook were put in his Party card. At the next enemy rush he hurriedly grabbed at his gun, but an enemy bullet got there first.

LETTERS FROM LAZAR PAPERNIK, ASSISTANT POLITICAL INSTRUCTOR OF A SKI DETACHMENT

LETTER TO HIS SISTER

Late December 1941

Dear little Zina and Leonard,

Happy New Year. Good luck and good health. I hope 1942 will be a year of happy homecomings after the fascist dogs have been kicked out of our land, so that we can all meet again in our dear Moscow.

As you can see from the papers, we are driving the nazi swine farther and farther from our Moscow, freeing more and more towns and villages. I've seen tens of people, young and old, children and old folk, greeting us with tears of happiness in their eyes.

I know the places we have been through in the past few days. I recalled the days I worked on building sites in the towns of Istra and New-Jerusalem; I well remember their buildings and museums. So it hurts me all the more, it really makes me boil, to see the way these monsters have smashed it all down, to see the way these plunderers have carried off everything of any value.

My dear ones, it's very difficult to get an idea from the papers of these nazi pigs and of their "New Order".

As assistant political instructor I have had enough opportunity to witness the consequences of the foul actions of the fascist scum. They're going to have to pay dearly for all they've done on our land. They'll have to answer for all the people they've enslaved.

1942 will be a year of complete destruction of these dregs of humanity, a year of destruction of everything born of the black plague of fascism.

I'm glad that in these difficult days I am among the country's defenders. I'm glad I've had a decent training for my service in the Red Army. All my peace-time hobbies—skiing, riding, shooting—have come in very handy and I proudly recall the days when, even though I was overloaded with work, I trudged off to the gliding school or to the Budyonny Cavalry School, and my days-off when I went skiing on the Vorobyovy Hills, even though mum was against it.

A couple of days ago I had a very interesting and touching meeting in the woods. After a nazi air raid, I was giving a hand to some comrades from the neighbouring unit, who had been raked by machine-gun fire, when I heard one of the wounded calling my name. Just imagine my surprise to see my old factory and riding school mate, Yasha.

Well, that's all, enjoy yourselves at the New Year. Best of luck, see you soon in Moscow.

Let me know the birthday of our little sisters, I remember it's somewhere between January 21 and 25. Let me know more exactly.

Yours,
Lazar

LETTER HOME

January 6, 1942

Dear Mum and Dad,

Alive, well, everything as before.

I'm doing as you wanted—killing the nazis and liberating the land for us and you, for thousands of people who have had to leave their homes.

Love and kisses,
Your Lazar

In January 1942, a group of skiers performed an act of bravery which was soon on the lips of every defender of Moscow. Twenty-three heroes fought and died but did not let the enemy through.

This is how it happened.

Under the blows of the Soviet forces the foe reeled back to the west, hanging on grimly to every village and hamlet. Bitter fighting occurred over the town of Sukhinichi which the nazis had turned into a stronghold.

The detachment of skiers in which Assistant Political Instructor Papernik was serving, received instructions to drive the nazis out of the village of Khludnevo and to hang on to it until the arrival of an infantry unit. It was absolutely vital to deprive the enemy of a footing here, this being a supply point for the main town defence.

During the night of January 23, twenty-five skiers made for the enemy posts. Under cover of darkness the detachment reached the village without any trouble. Here they found out from local inhabitants that nazi reinforcements of two light tanks, mortars and artillery had arrived in the village that evening. The two sides were rather unevenly matched: 25 Soviet soldiers to more than 400 Germans. Nevertheless the valiant few decided to do their duty at all costs.

Carefully spying out the enemy gun emplacements, the Soviet soldiers picked out their objects for attack.

It was already past midnight when the skiers came within striking distance and, at their commander's signal, simultaneously let fly their grenades and opened fire. The resultant panic gave the heroes a chance to pick off many enemy soldiers and to reach the centre of the village. But it was not long before the nazis came to their senses and began to fire back in earnest. Under cover of two tanks the Germans managed to press back the courageous men to the edge of the village. The detachment commander, Captain Laznyuk, was badly wounded. Political Instructor Yegortsev took command. He ordered one of the soldiers to carry the commander out of range of fire and then decided to make a dash with the remaining soldiers to a big timbered barn standing on a hill just beyond the village. Having taken up their places all round the barn, the skiers got ready to beat off the tanks. The enemies were closing in. The soldiers had to retreat into the barn. The fighting went on until morning.

Pravda of February 14, 1942, described this heroic epizode as follows:

"In the morning the mortars began to shell the barn.... One by one the skiers fell. The Germans wanted to take the rest prisoner, they stopped firing and closed in shouting: 'Surrender, Russ!' 'Soviet patriots never give themselves up!' someone shouted from the barn, and hand grenades exploded among the Germans followed by sub-machine-gun bursts. Enraged, the Germans threw all they had against the barn. Papernik was the only one left alive. The Germans made a rush intending to take at least one skier alive. 'Better death than nazi prison!' cried Papernik and blew himself up with a grenade."

When the village of Khludnevo was liberated, the villagers told the story of the heroic death of the skiers. Twenty-two heroes were posthumously awarded the Order of Lenin. For bravery and devotion to his country, Assistant Political Instructor Papernik was post-humously awarded the title of Hero of the Soviet Union.

Lazar Papernik was born in 1918 in a railwayman's family. From school he began work at the First Moscow Watch Factory, named after Kirov, first as turner then as milling-machine operator, adjuster, tool technician, controller and, finally, chief of the shop.

On July 17, 1941, Lazar Papernik volunteered for the front.

Lazar Papernik, Hero of the Soviet Union

APPEAL FROM IVAN BALABANOV
JUNIOR POLITICAL INSTRUCTOR
OF A MOTORISED BATTALION

January 28, 1942

Dear comrades,

I've done all I could. I took over command of the battalion after our commander had been wounded, and I continued the attack according to orders. I proudly looked death in the face because I have a Bolshevik heart. I am not afraid to die. I have fought hard because I love my people, my country and my Party.

As I die on the field of battle, I want to tell my comrades-in-arms that I have never known cowardice or panic.

My dying wish is that you destroy fascism once and for all. Be heroes of war so that history will remember you as valiant defenders of Russian land.

I hope that you, courageous Russian soldiers, will avenge my death.

Let my folks know how I lived and died.

Farewell, dear comrades-in-arms,

Ivan Balabanov

On January 28, 1942, Junior Political Instructor Balabanov led a group of soldiers in an attack on an enemy post in the village of Gusevo.

The enemy had firmly dug in. Every house, every barn had been turned into a stubborn nest of resistance. With the cry "Death to the nazi swine!" Balabanov, under heavy fire, rushed ahead of his soldiers to the nearest barn.

Though seriously wounded and losing blood, Balabanov forced his way into the barn. Stunned by the audacity of the attack, the enemy machine-gunners fled in panic.

The battle died down. As his strength began to ebb, Balabanov sensed that his hour was near. With shaking hands he took a sheet of paper from his map-case and wrote a few words to his comrades. Again the fighting flared up. The Soviet soldiers rushed forward again and again. The enemy was pushed back. His friends found Ivan Balabanov dead. In the cold hand of their beloved leader, the soldiers found a small sheet of paper—his last note.

Ivan Balabanov

LETTER
FROM SERGEANT YAKOV BONDAR
TO HIS UNIT PARTY ORGANISATION

I am glad to do my duty to liberate our country as quickly as possible from the German scourge. If I die, then I die a devoted patriot of my country, if I live I shall do all I can to defeat the enemy.

I love my country and am ready to shed my last drop of blood for her. One thing I know: the fascist beasts will soon be destroyed, and Soviet people will live even more happily than before.

Please consider me a Communist.

Sergeant Yakov Bondar, a Y.C.L. member, fought on the Leningrad Front. He was fatally wounded. In his pocket was this letter written on the eve of a battle.

TESTAMENT BY PRIVATE STEPAN VOLKOV

Not later than February 12, 1942

MY TESTAMENT

Comrade soldiers, commanders and political instructors,

As I go into attack, I pledge to fight to my last breath for the honour and independence of my country. I am not a Party member. But if I shed my blood in battle, consider it the blood of a Communist. Death and destruction to the nazi butchers who have sullied our sacred land!

Dear comrades-in-arms, if I die in this encounter, consider me a Communist.

Long live the great Soviet people.

Convey my greetings to my wife Marusya and daughter Tanya.

S. Volkov

Stepan Volkov served in a rifle company which had orders to attack enemy stronghold in the village of Ustinovo. Just before the attack, he wrote a pledge to his comrades. On a tiny piece of note-paper he hurriedly jotted down the words of his testament: to fight to the last breath against the nazi butchers. He rolled the note into a ball and put it inside his identity cylinder.

Volkov was one of the first in the attack. From a nazi trench ahead came a burst of fire. The attackers threw themselves flat. Stepan, grenades in his hands, crawled towards the German trench and threw in his grenades killing several Germans.

The enemy firing stopped. The way into the village of Ustinovo was free. But at that moment the fearless fighter was hit by an enemy bullet.

After the battle the soldiers buried Stepan Volkov on a hillock close to the village for whose liberation he had given his life. Over his grave they read out the note found on the hero.

NOTE FROM SOLDIER
ALEXANDER VINOGRADOV

There was a dozen of us sent down the Minsk Highway to bar the enemy's way, to stop the tanks. And we held out for all we could. Now only three of us are left: Kolya, Volodya and I, Alexander. But the enemy keeps coming on. There goes another—Volodya from Moscow. The tanks are coming at us. But 19 are already in flames along the road. Only two of us now. But we shall hold out as long as we can, we shan't let them by until our lads arrive.

Now there's only me, wounded in the head and arm. But we've knocked out more tanks. That makes 23 of them. Perhaps I'll die. But, maybe someone will someday find my note and remember us. I'm from Frunze, a Russian. No relatives. Farewell, friends.

> Yours,
> Alexander Vinogradov

> 22/2–1942

This note only came to light sixteen years later, in 1958, discovered by a carpenter from the Nekrasov State Farm in Uvarovsky District, Moscow Region. The carpenter, I. Smirnov, found it as he was squaring a birch log. The note had been scrawled in pencil on both sides of a narrow, thin strip of tracing paper.

In January and February 1942, the nazi High Command brought up another 40 divisions up from Germany and the occupied countries to the Soviet front to help stem the advance of the Soviet troops near Moscow. These reinforcements put Soviet troops fighting in the enemy rear in the region of Vyazma in a tight spot.

In the latter part of February, dogged battles flared up along the front of the 5th Army advancing on Gzhatsk. In mid-February, an order came through for the 612th Infantry Regiment of the 144th

Infantry Division of this army to push on into the enemy rear and cut off the nazi communications. The regiment advanced towards Gzhatsk and cut off the Minsk Highway almost 16 miles to the east of the town.

On February 20, 1942, the 612th Infantry Regiment was ordered to straddle the Minsk Highway 95 miles west of Moscow and block the way to the enemy tanks. The soldiers dug in along the highway. Alexander Vinogradov's group took up position on the right flank. The column of enemy tanks appeared all of a sudden speeding towards Moscow. The battalion put up a desperate resistance against the nazi tanks trying to blast their way through. For three days the infantrymen held out. Their ranks were thinning visibly, but no one gave way. Twice wounded Alexander Vinogradov wrote a last letter to his countrymen, squeezed it into a rifle cartridge and drove it into a tree trunk. When, on the fourth day of the encounter, the 612th Regiment men were relieved by units from the 108th Infantry Division only a handful of survivors remained.

TESTAMENT LETTER AND NOTE HOME
FROM LEONID SILIN

August 30, 1941-March 7, 1942

TESTAMENT LETTER

My dear ones at home,

Greetings, though when you read my letter I shall no longer be alive.

But through death, too, through my absence, I embrace you all, my dear ones, I kiss you. Not as a ghost but as your own live and dear daddie.

My boys and Anya, don't think I went away to this awful war out of some desire to cover myself in glory.

I knew I was probably going to my death.

I love life more than anything, but more than life I love you, Anya and my boys.

And knowing what terror, what humiliating torments awaited you if Hitler had his way, knowing how they would torture you, how they would treat your mother, knowing how your mother would shrivel up and you be turned into little skeletons, I, out of love for you, had to leave you, though wanting to be with you, had to go away to war.

I went to war, that means to my death, so that you may live.

These are no fancy words. For me these words are now clothed in flesh and blood, in my own blood.

My dear Annushka, I know you will have it hardest of all. I know. But for you to be safe I am going into the fire....

I have nothing else to add. Only to say there was no one else in the world I loved so much and found it so heartbreaking to leave behind for good, to leave behind alone, as you, my love.

Lenya, my elder son and helper,

We called you Lenya, like me.

So you will be me when I'm gone.

Our good, kind mummie has gone through a lot and dreamed so much of an easy peaceful life, but she never had much of a chance with me. I want you to make her happy.

I want her to find in you her best friend and helper. I realise it's not easy for children to grow up without a father, specially for boys. But, remember, I have died for you so that you lads can grow up—whether it be hard or not—so that you can grow up and not die from German bombs.

I have died as befits us men, defending our children, our wives, our homes, our land.

I want you too to live just as your dad lived and died.

Remember, your mum is my best friend, she's dearer to me than anyone else has ever been. So mum knows what's good and what's bad, what I've done and what I haven't, what I'd have approved of and what I wouldn't.

Always and in everything consult your mummie, don't hide anything from her, confide in all and share everything with her.

Never mind if she is a woman, she's a special woman, she's our mum, our beloved, clever mummie. She will understand everything.

Lenya, there's so much I must tell you, and I can't say it all, and a lot you won't understand anyway.

I have many things I'd like to tell you. But your mother will do this for me.

These are my parting words to you: don't forget your mum, Lenya Silin, look after her, see she is alright all her life. Love and obey your mum always.

Lenya Silin, my helper and elder son, farewell my little boy, and don't forget me.

Genya, my younger son and helper,

I leave you behind quite a toddler. You won't even remember your father's face or voice. But your elder brother, my elder son and helper, Lenya Silin, will tell you what your daddie was like, how much he loved you and what sort of man he was. Mum will let you know how your father lived, worked and struggled for a better life.

All I've written to your elder brother goes for you, too. If you listen to Lenya Silin and your mum I'm sure you will be a good, brave and decent man.

My boys Lenya and Genya,

Work well at school, study German very carefully, German culture and German sciences. And you must use it all to defeat and destroy German fascism.

Try to learn from the Germans their most dangerous and terrible weapon—their organisation and precision.

And, when you feel you are strong enough, use all you have against the nazis. Don't forget, my sons, as long as nazi Germany remains, as long as one armed nazi remains, as long as even one nazi laboratory or factory carries on unchecked, then Europe, the world, mankind and you personally, and your mummie, your wives and children will live in mortal, terrible danger.

Never forget: fascism in general, and German fascism in particular, is a deadly, ravaging leprosy, the black plague, which threatens all mankind.

May your father's blood, may your father's ashes be a reminder to your little hearts, my lads, and may the last armed nazi feel your terrible revenge.

My boys and Anya, the main thing without me is to keep calm and organise your life in an orderly way, no matter what you do.

We, and myself in particular, came to grief because of the stupid and cocksure system of leaving everything to chance, disgusting organisation and the cackle-handedness of certain commanders who haven't got the faintest idea about modern war and underestimate the enemy.

I believe the enemy will be smashed and we shall win. If not, destroy the enemy wherever and whenever you have the chance.

Boys, listen to our dear, beloved mummie. She means everything to me, my nearest and dearest.

Annushka, my dear one, farewell!

My darling, my honey,

Bring up our sons so that I would be proud of them even though I'm not there, so that I would be pleased with my strong, brave and optimistic lads, terrors of the foe and tender and kind to people.

Be happy and healthy, look after yourselves.

Farewell, love and kisses for the last time. To you, Gena, you, Lenya, you, Anya. Farewell!

Yours,

Dad

Forever Yours,

Lenya Silin—Senior
August 30, 1941

NOTE

My dear wife Anna and boys Lenya and Gennady,

I want to hug and kiss you for the last time. Today I am to be shot by order of the German Command.

Boys, grow up and get your own back on all fascists for me. As I part from you I am entrusting you with all my blessed hatred for these vile swine. Cut them down to the last fascist. I've lived honourably, fought honourably and die honourably.

I die for our country, for our Party, for all Russians, Ukrainians, Byelorussians and all other people in the country, and for you. Love our country like I love her, fight for her like I have and, if need be, die for her like me.

Boys, love and respect and obey your mother, she's going to have a hard time bringing you up, but our country and comrades whom I've saved, won't leave you in the lurch. Remember every soldier must have one motto: I die but don't surrender. I didn't surrender. I had a concussion, couldn't walk and it wasn't right to desert my badly wounded companions. When we were prisoners I set up a Soviet colony and saved many lives. I stood by them to the last minute, I've done all I could for my country. Time's running out.

My dear ones, be decent Soviet people, grow up to be Bolsheviks! Anna, farewell! Lenya and Gennady, good-bye!
Long live our country!

All my love,
Your husband and father

Leonid Silin

Leonid Silin joined up in the early days of the war. He came from a Riga family, his father being a minor official. He grew up in the same district as several German families and so came to have a good knowledge of German. Before the war he served in the Navy at Sevastopol, then worked at the Moscow Bearing Works and took a correspondence course in the Moscow College of Law. Because of a weak heart he was exempted from army service but he was one of the first to sign up when war broke out, hiding his health record. But the doctors found this out and he was discharged. It would have taken more than that to keep Leonid Silin out of action. He succeeded in his second attempt to get to the front, this time as a lawyer.

These were trying years for the Soviet Union. Three months of war had brought the enemy half-way through the Ukraine. Silin's unit could not hold onto the right bank of the Dnieper and in September 1941 had to beat a retreat to Poltava. A large group of badly wounded soldiers was cut off and had to hole out in the village of Krestitelevo. The wounded lay in long barns and listened to the roar of the fighting. Finally they heard German speech. What were they to do? The enemy was likely to burn down the barns thus murdering dozens of wounded. A decision was taken in a flash. Leonid Silin rose from the straw, opened the barn door and, limping badly and leaning on a crutch, went out of the barn.

In faultless German he called out to the Germans that there were only badly wounded soldiers in the barns and asked them to hold their fire. The sudden appearance of a Soviet officer speaking fluent German took the sergeant-major by surprise and the firing stopped. Silin was taken to headquarters.

Back at H.Q., Silin endeavoured to prove himself before the senior German officers a German sympathiser. He praised the German successes and requested only that he be permitted to organise a hospital for wounded Soviet prisoners-of-war (he put himself forward as a wounded Soviet doctor). He knew full well what to expect if the Germans got wind of his complete medical ignorance. But he had to save people and it was well worth the risk. The Germans seemed pleased with the "doctor", so smart and excellently versed in German. They gave him permission to set up what passed as a hospital.

From among his fellow prisoners, Silin selected a group of surgeons, nurses and orderlies for his staff. Thus came into being Silin's

"Ukrainian" hospital. The nazis refused to allow any wounded Soviet officers, Communists, Jews or Russians here. And so the staff had to disguise every new entry under a Ukrainian name.

In November the occupational forces gave permission for the hospital to be moved to the village of Yeremeyevka where it was housed in a big, two-storey school. Now the wounded had a roof over their heads and there was more food to go round as the village was some distance off the beaten track, which meant less frequent raids from German requisitioning officials.

Leonid Silin was playing for time to allow the wounded to get back their strength, hoping some time later to escape from the hospital in a body and join up with the partisans in the woods. The medical staff began to engage in underground activities. They managed to get hold of a receiver and listened in to Sovinformbureau news, which they passed on to the rest of the hospital and the villagers as well. From the German stores sacks of corn began to disappear and policemen would misplace their rifles and submachineguns.

So as not to bring down the wrath of the nazis on the hospital, Silin and his confederates had to be extremely careful. Nevertheless, the German-appointed senior police officer of Yeremeyevka, the traitor Atamas, nicknamed the "Dragon", sensed that Silin was playing a double game. Wanting to curry favour with the Germans, Atamas began to watch Silin and gather evidence. One of the hospital staff also turned traitor.

On the night of March 2, 1942, the hospital was surrounded by German soldiers and Ukrainian police. The nazis subjected all the patients to a thorough examination and found that some were quite fit and also that there was quite a number of Russians and Jews. This discovery meant death for the hospital staff. On the next day, March 3, about 40 wounded and doctors picked out by the Germans, were taken from the hospital to the Kremenchug p.o.w. camp.

Leonid Silin remained courageous to the end. As he was being led out to the sleighs on which the wounded lay, he asked leave to bid farewell to those remaining. Addressing the villagers gathered on the village square and his wounded comrades, he called on them to continue the struggle against the invaders and keep faith in the victory of the Red Army. Seeing the enormous effect his speech was having on the people, the German officer cut him short and refused him further time. As the sleigh started to move Leonid Silin bit through a vein in his wrist, soaked his handkerchief in blood and, throwing it into the crowd, cried: "See it gets to my sons."

The brave Riga man was shot on March 7, 1942, together with doctors Portnov and Gekker, a wounded Lieutenant-Colonel K. Bogoroditsky and others.

A day later, an escapee from the Kremenchug camp brought Silin's note to Oksana Romanchenko, a nurse at the hospital. He had managed to write it before he was shot and pass it on to some comrades with the request to get it through to nurse Romanchenko. The note was written in pencil on sheets of paper and addressed to his wife and children. When Soviet forces liberated Yeremeyevka, nurse Romanchenko dispatched the note to the Moscow address indicated.

LAST ISSUE
OF A HANDWRITTEN NEWSSHEET "OKOPNAYA PRAVDA" PUBLISHED BY YOUNG PIONEER VALERI VOLKOV

Beginning of 1942

Our handful of men are a mighty force which the enemy reckons a division. . . .

. . . No power in the world can defeat us, Soviet people, because we are our own masters, led by our Communist Party.

This is who we are. . . .

Here, in School No. 52:

1. Commander . . . Zhidilov, Russian;
2. Cavalry Captain Gobaladze, Georgian;
3. Tank man, Vasili Paukshtite, Lett;
4. . . . Captain-Surgeon Mamedov, Uzbek;
5. Pilot, Junior Lieutenant Ilita Daurova, an Ossetian girl;
6. Sailor Ibrahim Ibrahimov, Kazan Tatar;
7. Gunner Petrunenko from Kiev, Ukrainian;
8. Infantry Sergeant Bogomolov from Leningrad, Russian;
9. Diver-scout Arkady Zhuravlev from Vladivostok;
10. I, son of a cobbler, 4th form pupil, Valeri Volkov, Russian. . . .

Dear comrades,

Whoever gets out of this alive must tell all who will study at this school. No matter where you end up come and tell them what happened here in Sevastopol. I want to be a bird and fly round all Sevastopol, to every home, every school, every street.... Hitler and the other scum will never beat us.... We are the millions, watch out! From the Far East to Riga, from the Caucasus to Kiev, from Sevastopol to Tashkent.... We, like steel, are invincible!

Valeri "the Poet" (Volk)
1942

This small newssheet was written to the accompaniment of the thunder of battle by a 13-year-old Sevastopol schoolboy, Valeri Volkov, one of the heroic defenders of the besieged city.

Valeri fought among the grown-ups acting as lookout, scouting and bringing in ammunition, assisting the wounded and using his rifle when the Germans attacked. Those were fierce battles with no quarter given day or night. Only eight men, a woman and a boy were left, four Russians, a Ukrainian, a Georgian, a Lett, an Uzbek, a Tatar and an Ossetian girl. That is when issue No. 11, the last, of their own newspaper came out—a vivid testament to the courage of the heroic ten.

Tanks were bearing down on the heroes. They tossed their grenades. Valeri blew up one of the tanks. But the young hero was the victim of an enemy bullet.

Twenty years went by and the ten Sevastopol heroes remained unknown. It was only recently that two of the survivors, Ivan Petrunenko and woman pilot Ilita Daurova, brought the last newssheet to people's notice.

NOTE FROM YEVGENIA BAGRECHEVA, SECRETARY OF UNDERGROUND PARTY ORGANISATION, TO HER MOTHER

Not later than March 19, 1942

Good-bye, my dear Mummie and Eleonora. As I wait to be hanged I am writing to send my last greetings.

Don't cry, Mum, and don't say it's my own fault. There was no other way. Look after yourself for Ellie's sake, you should now be both grannie and mother to her. Bring her up a good girl and a kind person, see that she loves her country and people.

All my love to you all, remember me to all our relations, friends and my pupils, all those who manage to get through this awful time.

Zhenya

Yevgenia Bagrecheva

They all respected her in Kardymovo, the district centre of the Smolensk Region, where she was history teacher in the local secondary school. They respected her for her love for children, her pleasant air, modesty and because she was exacting to herself and her comrades.

In Kardymovo, as everywhere else in the country, the Germans came up against well-organised resistance. Yevgenia was secretary of the village Communists; her fellow resistance fighters were I. Kovalev, Chairman of the Kardymovo Village Soviet, M. Selyaninova, schoolmistress, P. Shesterikova, doctor, I. Kutsenko, from a district hospital, and others.

A strong partisan movement swept the whole Smolensk Region. No small thorn in the nazis' side was provided by the Kardymovo people. After the first winter of the war, Soviet power was, in fact, restored in several villages. To put down partisan resistance, the German Command sent in its crack units from the 10th Tank Division. The nazis burned down 25 villages, shot and hanged over 500 people and carted off hundreds to their prisoner-of-war camp in Smolensk.

On March 19, 1942, Yevgenia Bagrecheva was hanged in the village centre. Before her death, she had been tortured for a long time. But nothing had broken her spirit. A few hours before her death she wrote her last letter on a tiny scrap of paper. It is now preserved in the Smolensk State Museum.

LETTER AND INSCRIPTION
WRITTEN BY RZHEV UNDERGROUND WORKERS
ALEXEI ZHILTSOV AND ALEXANDER BELYAKOV

Not later than March 28, 1942

LETTER FROM ALEXEI ZHILTSOV TO HIS FATHER

My dear Dad,

Don't cry. Don't worry. Your son will never let anyone down. If you keep alive let others know about us. I don't want to die—so little we've done.

INSCRIPTION MADE BY ALEXANDER BELYAKOV
ON THE WALL OF HIS CELL

I shall endure all their inhuman torture. I give you my word as a Komsomol member, dear comrades, they will never make me talk. And don't you talk either. The great things we have begun will be carried through by our comrades.

An underground Y.C.L. was formed in the city of Rzhev in the first months of nazi occupation. It was led by Alexei Teleshov. There were ten in the group in October 1941.

The youngsters were not long in establishing contact with the partisans in the Panin woods. Numbers quickly multiplied. In order to get their hands on weapons, the young fighters would dispose of the German sentries. They also made a raid on the ammunition dump. Their exploits began to get around among the soldiers fighting on the Kalinin Front. In November 1941, Vladimir Novozhenov, a scout from one of the army units, established contact with them. They now began to indicate targets for Soviet bombers, made raids on enemy transports and blew up railway tracks.

Their activities were cut short by a betrayal. Fifteen underground members were rounded up.

After excruciating torture, there was a public hanging of Teleshov, Novozhenov and Belyakov on March 28, 1942. The rest were shot.

Before he died Alexei Zhiltsov managed to get a letter through to his father. On the wall of the town dungeon was later found the inscription made by Alexander Belyakov.

Alexei Zhiltsov

LETTER
FROM PYOTR TSURANOV, SECRETARY
OF DUKHOVSHCHINA UNDERGROUND DISTRICT
PARTY COMMITTEE, TO HIS WIFE

April 3, 1942

Dear Vera, my darling, my own little dove,

My heart leaps with joy just to think you may get my letter, you and our boy and girl will see my writing and know I am alive and well.

We haven't seen or heard anything of each other for over nine months. Now, when I have a chance to send you a letter there's so much I want to tell you, so much. . . .

What can I say to you? I remember, all my life I'll remember Kulagino where I saw you (July 15) when you were sick, with our newborn girl, where we parted so suddenly, without saying good-bye properly. But I knew you couldn't be angry at me, both as my wife and friend, since duty compelled me to stay in the district come what may. I can well imagine the whole horror of the situation in which I left you. Yet, as you know, there was nothing I could do to help. I consoled myself with the one thought that your suffering is all our people's suffering, that there are thousands of martyrs like you, that war is war.

But what is wonderful, my sweet, is that I haven't for one moment lost my confidence that you are alive, that you think about me, that you love me, as you did ten years ago, as you always loved me. Not for one minute have I lost faith in us seeing each other again, in being together again. And I still believe it now, as much as I believe in our victory over Hitler's bandits.

My darling, my little dove, we'll be together again. Just wait and see. Keep your spirits up. I shall live yet to hug and kiss you all! I'm longing for that wonderful moment as much as I do for our country's complete liberation from the fascist scum. That moment is coming nearer. We are all sure of it, we Bolsheviks, partisans and all the people in our district.

Nine months in the nazi rear—how have I lived, where have I lived in this time? How have we fought against the German invaders? It cannot be described all in one letter.

No matter what I write to you it would still seem a trifle.

The first weeks and months of underground work were very grim. We have now about ten detachments in the district. I'm not exactly sure how many men we have in each detachment; in my lot there are over a hundred. They're a wonderful, select bunch.

I've been living in Fyodorovo, Ponizovye, Grishkovo, Petrishchevo and Bosino. I've had to spend my nights in the fields and woods. All autumn I was with a group of comrades in the woods. February I lived in a dug-out. Can't grumble about my health. I've probably never felt better. My stomach ulcer seems to have healed, cicatrised. However much I hid, the Dukhovshchina gang—those fascist creeps—soon nosed me out. They've been hunting me like a bear, but it hasn't got them anywhere. Only one ...* and several times we've led them a merry dance. The Germans' fate in Demidovo, Prechistoye and Dukhovshchina will be decided in a few days. For the moment though we are still behind the lines, surrounded by the foe, but they cannot do a thing about us. The partisans are like quicksilver. Right from the beginning things have been fine, marvellous. What's wonderful is that all the people round here are right behind us, assisting us and hating the nazis.

What more is there to tell you? When I was left in the district I combed the whole area far and wide. I roped in almost all Communists. I organised them in underground Party partisan groups. Now they have grown into partisan detachments. In one of these I am commissar. . . .

A few of our good comrades fell into German hands and lost their lives. I, as you see, with some fifty local Communists have survived. Some of them have been with the partisans since autumn, others since winter.

---

* Text is rubbed out here in the paper's fold.

Now Dukhovshchina is surrounded by partisan detachments. We've made short work of all nazi appointees. No one nazi-appointed administration body is now operating. For the time being the Germans are holing out like wolves in Dukhovshchina and a few other villages. In a number of villages we have already restored Soviet power. In the rest power [also] belongs to the partisans. My oh my, how the nazis are scared of the partisans...* and I've easily escaped their clutches. Well, now I think they haven't got a chance.

My dear little dove, I must hurry. I haven't written even a fraction of what I wanted. Farewell.

Take care, bring up our son and little girl. I hope they are clever and good, I hope they grow up Bolsheviks. I hope they, and you as well, love our country.... And never lose faith in our deliverance from the enemy.

Many, many kisses to you all.

No matter what happens to me I'm sure you'll be brave and come through all the hardships and, at least, bring up our son Volodya and daughter Nelya. If only I could see them now. I can just imagine them. Remember how we used to go on a ramble with our little girl? I haven't got anything more to write on. Farewell.... Kisses....

Yours and yours alone,
Pyotr

Pyotr Tsuranov, second secretary of the Dukhovshchina District Party Committee, was in charge of underground work in the district. Under his leadership several underground groups were formed, followed by small partisan units. With one of the units he took to the woods neighbouring on Kasplyansky District. Here the partisan ranks were reinforced by soldiers left behind in the rear and also by the villagers.

Back in early September 1941, this unit had taken part in skirmishes with regular units of the 9th German Army, thereby rendering active assistance to the Soviet Army.

At the commencement to 1942, the unit had its base in the village of Grishkovo, and a couple of months later in Gorodnya. It was joined there by other partisan groups and detachments.

On March 25, 1942, a band of partisans headed by Pyotr Tsuranov waited in ambush near the village of Zakup to which a column of 300

---

* Another omission due to erasure in the letter's fold.

German soldiers was heading. The partisans scattered the Germans who fled in panic leaving behind more than a hundred dead.

Pyotr wanted to tell his wife of the hazards of fighting behind the lines and the first thrills of their modest victories. This letter of April 3rd is their first contact since parting. Will it get through to her? Will his family know he is alive and well? Hardly having time to send the letter he rushed off again into the fray, this time in the village of Falisa held by police collecting taxes from the population. Tsuranov and his companions blasted the nazis from the village with hand grenades and eventually drove them out of Trofimenka and Voskresenskoye too. The clashes lasted two days.

Pyotr Tsuranov

In April and May, a number of districts around Smolensk were freed by the partisans and Soviet authority was restored. On May Day there was a meeting of the Dukhovshchina underground District Party Committee Bureau which discussed ways and means of getting the whole district back into Soviet hands. District Party Secretary Pyotr Tsuranov was responsible for this work throughout the district. The Bureau, jointly with the District Party Executive Committee and the Y.C.L. Committee, addressed the following appeal to the people:

"Soviet power has been restored and Soviet authority is now coming into its own on the territory of our district liberated from the nazis, i.e., in 10 village Soviets. But the battle against the foe certainly does not end here. Our victories have to be consolidated and taken further. We must do all we can to assist the Red Army and red partisans to smash the enemy and drive Hitler's hordes out of the Soviet Union.

"We shall win!"

On June 22, an anti-fascist meeting of people from all over the district took place. The resolution adopted by 500 delegates and signed by Pyotr Tsuranov ended with slogans: "Long live our Soviet homeland!" "Down with the fascist scum!"

In the summer of 1942, after a round of bitter fighting, the district was occupied for the second time. Pyotr was put in charge of the Burevestnik partisan unit and once more never gave himself any let-up in fearless raids on the nazis, organising underground operations, sabotage and raids.

In February 1943, the bold Communists' leader of Dukhovshchina made his last sortie.

LETTERS FROM YELENA UBIIVOVK, UNDERGROUND Y.C.L. WORKER IN POLTAVA, FROM A GESTAPO CELL

LETTER TO HER FATHER

12-13 May, 1942

Dear Dad,

You are a man and must take everything that comes as a man. I have one chance in a hundred of getting out alive. Sergei isn't to blame—he's done all he could to save me.

I'm not writing in a scatter-brained mood. I've given it a lot of thought. As long as my breath holds out I shan't give up hope. But if I die, this is my last wish: mum, I know, won't get over my death, but you must live and get revenge whenever you can.

From here, from the very heart of fascism, I clearly see what this craven bestiality actually is.

I'm not afraid of death, but I want, if there is no other way out, to die by my own hand. That is why I appeal to all that you hold sacred, to your love for me—to bring me some opium today—we have some at home in a bottle, exactly the amount I need, no more no less, so as not to miss.

I know you'll do it for the love of me. Don't forget I'm not scatter-brained and won't do anything rash. Pour it into a phial and put it in a loaf. Better in a pot of soup, I can tip the soup out.

I'll do my duty—I shan't implicate any innocent people and, if need be, I'll die bravely.

But, to release me from my torturers, get it to me today, while you can still visit me, a fatal dose of opium or morphia —I realise you know best so be a good dad so that I don't have to suffer any more. By 5 o'clock I'll be taken down to the prison where you can see me.

Let my friends know I'm confident my death will be avenged. Valya is a traitress, she split on me and Sergei. Sergei's a good lad. Don't forget to let them know all this.

My every word is my last wish and my mind will be at peace if I find you've done everything.

I still have hope, but my decision stands firm if all hope fades. Don't tell mum anything for the time being.

Love to you all from the bottom of my heart.

Greetings to friends

LETTER HOME

May 20, 1942

Greetings to you all at home,

I cannot write much but want to send you all my best regards. I'm quite all right here. I get all the things you send in, except scent. If you want to send me something—scent or cigarettes—bring it to the prison where there's less control.

My chances of getting out of here are very, very slim. I shan't give up all hope of course, if I manage it I'll get out. But I shan't buy my life at the price of treachery. After all we only die once and life isn't all that is worthwhile these days, I see it very clearly here.

I'm very, very sorry I have to cause you so much worry. Believe you me, I've never forgotten you and never shall.

I get enough to eat with the food you send, but bread is short. . . . Why, dad, didn't you send what I asked? You know I've never done anything rash and never lose my head.

Now I feel alright and keep worrying only about you. Don't forget, Sergei is not in any way, not in the slightest, to blame —he did all he could and more even to save me. It's the circumstances that are to blame, they don't meet our wishes.

I suppose I made a stupid mistake in telling about the Y.C.L. Well, it can't be helped. Now, naturally, I'm looking for a way of getting out (except treachery). They treat me well, decently, better than the others. But that's nothing to go by.

Lots of love to you all. Love to Mum, Dad, Verochka, Glafira, Anyuta, Lelya and Igor.

May 23, 1942

My dear ones,

I'm very sorry I have to grieve you so. And I'm very sorry you don't understand me at all. My life just couldn't be any different in these circumstances. So it's necessary for death to bring some kind of good. Remember the cost of "repentance"? Futile humility blotting out the past, and it won't save lives anyway.

Dad, we were really together the whole day September 17. They're very crafty here. How could you, a grown man, be so trusting. You can give me away completely by being too trusting. They use the most subtle means of getting what they want. It wasn't out of humanism they let you see me. It's impossible to describe it. You have to be here and see it all to be convinced with your own eyes.

I have, and believe this, from what they say, a very small chance of getting out of here, and I'll do all I can to make use of it. And as far as treachery goes—that's another method they use. I've read Sergei's testimony—he didn't give me away, not by a single word.

By trying to cause trouble between us they aim at doing more damage. I signed the testimony. It's just as well I know a bit of German. What about those who don't? And you believe these people. . . . You shouldn't. I shall naturally try to keep alive. But if I don't succeed, you must get revenge for me. I'm not afraid to die—everyone has to die some time. But if I have to die, it's going to be the way the maximum good comes out of it. Just believe me and not them. I'm fighting for my life and know what I'm doing; it's easier for me here to see what to do than for you on the outside. I am no child and could have proved it to you.

Lots of love to all of you from the bottom of my heart.

Lyalya

LETTER HOME

May 24-25, 1942

Dear Mum, Dad, Verochka and Glafira,

Today, tomorrow—I don't know when—they are going to shoot me because I cannot go against my conscience, because I am a Komsomol girl. I'm not afraid to die. I shall die calmly.

I know full well that I cannot get out of here. Believe me I'm not writing in a hot-headed way. I'm quite cool and collected. Love and many kisses to you all for the last time. I'm not lonely and I feel a lot of love and concern around me. It's not so terrible to die.

Love to you all from the bottom of my heart.

Lyalya

Yelena Ubiivovk was a Y.C.L. member and student at Kharkov University. The war found her in Poltava.

During the occupation of Poltava several young people's underground organisations were formed.

Yelena set up an underground group which started up with nine Y.C.L. members. Together with her companions she collected weapons and conducted anti-fascist propaganda among the townsmen. The underground workers managed to get in contact with a partisan unit under the command of Zharov who was operating in the woods. The Y.C.L.-ers began to regularly take down news from Moscow over the radio and put out leaflets on behalf of the partisans. In six months they had circulated over two thousand leaflets. The group grew to twenty.

The young patriots used to lend a hand to the p.o.w.s in a Poltava prison camp, supplying them with civilian clothing and food. They helped eighteen prisoners escape and get through to the partisans. The Y.C.L. group was preparing for a suitable moment to instigate an armed uprising in Poltava.

Due to too much trust in the townspeople, the group was uncovered. On May 6, 1942, the leading members were arrested and tortured.

Yelena Ubiivovk was interrogated twenty-six times. On May 26, before sunset, after bravely withstanding all kinds of torture Yelena Ubiivovk, Sergei Sapega, Boris Serga, Sergei Ilyevsky, Valentin Soroka and Leonid Puzanov were shot beyond the Poltava town cemetery. Before she died Yelena managed to get four letters smuggled out of the Gestapo dungeon to her parents.

Yelena Ubiivovk

FROM THE DIARY OF IVAN MEDVEDOVSKY, MEMBER OF UNDERGROUND ORGANISATION IN THE VILLAGE OF CHAPAYEVKA

End of May 1942

They crucified me like Jesus Christ. They beat me with sticks and ramrods, stuck needles into me.

May 3, 1942. Yesterday had a session with the S.D. Let go for now. Live in stinking conditions. No bread, potatoes, nothing. Beginning to swell. Bruises pain me, all the same want to live. Live for the future.

Ivan Medvedovsky

When the Soviet Army retreated eastwards, underground groups were formed in the Zaporozhye Region. One such group was formed in the village of Chapayevka under the leadership of the local headmaster Ivan Medvedovsky, a Y.C.L. member. He conducted a campaign among the villagers and taught the young people how to combat the nazi invaders.

In May 1942, he was arrested for the fourth time by the Gestapo and shot.

Just before he met his end he got his last note through to his wife in which he expressed his profound faith in Soviet victory. "For all the vile deeds, the people of our country will pay the fascist swine back in full. The time is not far off when bloodthirsty Hilter and his gang will be wiped off the face of the earth."

VOW BY JUNIOR SERGEANT
VASILY AZAROV

I, son of my Homeland, brought up among the working people, vow to defend my Naval fortress on the Black Sea–Sevastopol–bravely and use my rifle to the best of ability.

I shall kill as many enemies as I can and part with my life as dearly as possible. After fighting off two enemy attacks we shall fight off the third too and completely rout them.

5.06.42. V. Azarov

Vasily Azarov was born in 1919. He fell in action while fending off the third and most desperate nazi drive on Sevastopol in June 1942.

About this time the combat around Sevastopol had reached its climax. Endeavouring to quickly overrun the key Soviet naval base on the Black Sea, Hitler's High Command hurled 11 divisions–over 300,000 fighting men–against the port's defenders. Enemy forces were backed up by 400 tanks, 2,000 guns and more than 500 planes. Taking advantage of their overwhelming superiority, the nazis tore into the town from land and air.

Cut off from their land communications and having great difficulty in obtaining military supplies and provisions, the Soviet soldiers, sailors and townsmen accomplished wonders of gallantry and heroism.

The defence of Sevastopol was of immense military and political significance. By diverting a vast number of German and Rumanian troops, the defenders foiled the German High Command's plans. Through their astonishing grit and fortitude, the Sevastopol men gave the enemy far more than he expected and dealt shattering blows to his manpower and armaments.

Defence of the port lasted for 250 heroic days, of which every one bore its own tale of valour. Few came out alive. But their names are forever inscribed on the roll of the war's bravest defenders.

The courageous words written by Vasily Azarov show the indomitable spirit of the Soviet fighters for the fortress of the Black Sea.

LETTERS
FROM TWO GOMEL UNDERGROUND MEN—
IVAN SHILOV AND TIMOFEI BORODIN

LETTER FROM IVAN SHILOV

My dear Mum, Dad and brothers,

I am now in prison. The charges appear to be very serious—
it looks like the end of the road. There we are. Can't do
anything about it. I'm not the first and probably shan't be the
last.... So I beg you not to take it too badly. I love you all,
dearest mum and dad, my wife, little girl, and I love my
country. If this letter ever gets through to my family, I hope
it will remind you of the last days of my life. Survived at
the front but not at home. Fair enough, but I don't want any
of my family to grieve over it....

Today was the first interrogation. The next is on Monday,
11/5, when they'll give me the works. I only fear that my
arrest will make things hard for you. That's all for today. If
I get the chance I'll write some more. Good-bye for now,
love to all.

Yours,

Vanya

May 9, 1942

LETTER FROM TIMOFEI BORODIN

My dear ones,

Writing you in my last hour. Looks like I'll have my lot
from a bullet.

Mum, Dad, Valya, Tonya, Lida, Nina, Zhenya, Volodya,
Arkady, Sasha—if I've ever been unfair to any of you please

forgive me. My dear ones, look after yourselves and don't ever quarrel.

Dad, look after Tonya and Sasha. Greetings in my last hour to all at home and all the folks I know.

Borodin Timofei
20-VI-42.

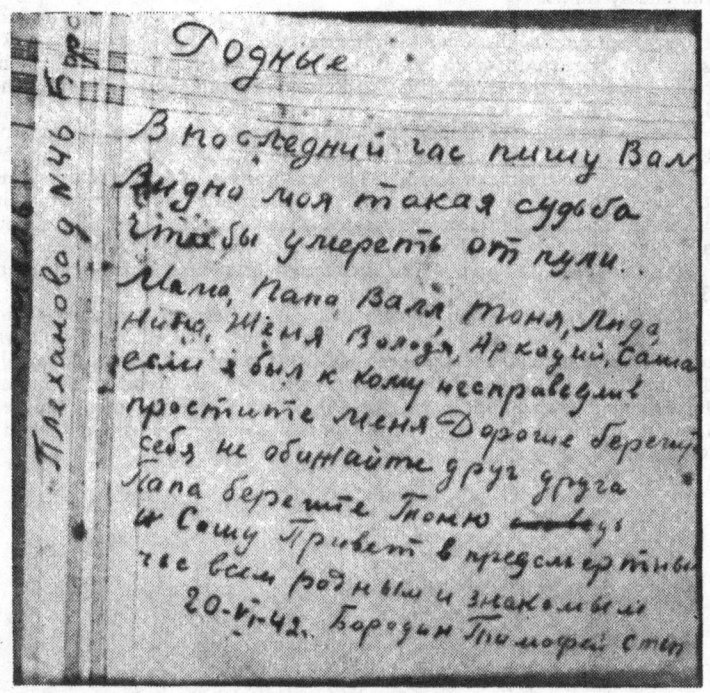

Borodin's letter on a handkerchief

In the second half of August 1941, the Gomel Region of Byelorussia was occupied by the Germans. By autumn an underground Party and Y.C.L. organisation was in full swing. It was headed by Communist Roman Timofeyenko and Y.C.L. members Timofei Borodin and Ivan Shilov.

Timofei Borodin had been working in a printer's. After the Germans had entered the town he went underground.

Ivan Shilov served in the Soviet Army. Soon after the outbreak of war he had been caught in a German ring, but managed to get back to his native Gomel where he, too, joined the underground. Being an expert at German he disguised himself as a German officer and operated within the nazi ranks.

One had to have an ineradicable faith in victory to be able to scorn death and boldly take on such a dangerous task right under the enemy's nose.

The underground fighters riddled the occupational machine and together with the partisans disrupted the invaders' economic, political and administrative measures, thereby sowing uncertainty and fear in the enemy ranks.

At the commencement to 1942, members of the underground turned their attention on the town's industrial works. They blew up workshops in the engineering plant where the Germans repaired their tanks, wrecked the locomotive works and knocked out several trainloads of arms and ammunition.

On the territory of Gomel Region the best sons and daughters of the Byelorussian people took up arms in dogged partisan combat against the occupational forces. The partisans worked in close contact with the town's underground. Fighters inside the town got their hands on medical supplies and passed them on to the partisans. They also kept them supplied with arms, ammunition and explosives.

In May 1942, the two Y.C.L. members Timofei Borodin and Ivan Shilov were given away and arrested.

Horrible tortures began. To no avail. The Gestapo promised them their lives if they were to name their fellow underground fighters and tell where to locate the partisan detachments. Again to no avail. The patriots would not split on their comrades. On June 20, Timofei Borodin and Ivan Shilov were shot. One hour before he died Timofei Borodin wrote his last note in big letters on his blood-stained handkerchief.

NOTE AND VOW
FROM Y.C.L. SIGNALMAN
VLADIMIR PANKEVICH

Not later than July 23, 1942

I swear to you, Vera, that I, a son of the people, will pound the enemy to my last gasp, to my last drop of blood. My love for you has remained and multiplied many times.

Vladimir Pankevich spared no effort to keep communications going for the forward sections of his unit, even though he constantly had to run a gauntlet of withering fire. When it came to furious battle for the villages of Solnechnogorsk, Volokolamsk and others, he was a brave example to others. He was struck down in the fighting for the village of Bykovo. In his pocket they found a photo and this unsent note to his girl-friend Vera.

LETTER
FROM YAKOV GORDIENKO
OF THE ODESSA UNDERGROUND

Dear Mum and Dad,

I'm writing you my last note. 27-VII-42. That makes exactly a month from the day they passed sentence. My time is running out, and perhaps I won't live till next letter. I don't expect any mercy. These rats know full well who I am (thanks to the swine who gave me away). At the inquest I kept pretty cool. I refused to answer. They took me away for beatings. Three times they took me and beat me up for about four to five hours. At half past three they stopped beating me. In that time I lost consciousness three times and once I made as if I had fainted. They beat me with a rubber hose, braided with a thin wire. Then with a wooden stick, about five feet long. Iron rods on my arms. . . . After that battering I still have the scars on my legs and higher up. Now I can't hear very well.

The rest of the boys in my group needn't worry. No torture could tear their names from me. I led the boys on the job. I gathered information. I was going to blow up a house where the Gerries were (a new building next to the Red Army House). But the old geezer putting me up got the wind up. He knew if I'd got hold of the bloke that gave me away I would have throttled him. I'd already done one bloke in. Shame I didn't have enough time. . . .

I reckoned on escaping. But a couple of days ago some criminals here were going to make a break and they were

72

found out. Now there's no chance of getting out and there's not much time left. Keep your end up. Sasha Khoroshenko swore he wouldn't leave you in the lurch if anything happened to me. You can bet your boots he'll be out. He has time and he'll pick his moment to make a break. Our cause will win all the same. The Soviets will mop up the Gerries and corn-chewing "liberators" this winter. They'll get it back a thousand times worse for the blood of the partisans shot by these bastards. I'm just sorry I won't be able to help my companions when the time comes.

See if you can get hold of my documents. They're buried in the shed. About a foot down under the first board from the whetstone. There you'll find photos of my pals and companions and my Y.C.L. card. The sigurantsa couldn't get it out of me that I'm in the Y.C.L.

There's a photo of Vova F., please take it to 7 Lutheransky Lane, to Nina Georgievna. Take it to her and tell her to make a copy, and take the photo back. Maybe you'll meet him one day. My letters are also there. And a box too. You can open it. There is a vow inside, a vow of eternal friendship and solidarity to each other. But we found ourselves all over the place. I'm condemned to be shot. Vova, Misha and Abrasha have been evacuated. They were wonderful chaps though. Maybe you'll come across some of them.

Good-bye Mum and Dad. Get well soon, Dad. That's what I want. Just ask you not to forget us and to get your own back on the rats who gave us away. Give my regards to Lena.

Lots of love to you all. Don't lose heart. Keep your ends up. Best wishes to all the family. Victory will be ours!

27.VII.42.

Yasha

During the heroic days of the Odessa defence in August 1941, a stocky figure turned up in Captain Molodtsov's "flying detachment". He was given a signaller's job. It was sixteen-year-old Yasha Gordienko. The young lad dreamed of great feats and burned to get hold of a gun to defend his home town from the nazi invaders. But the soldiers kept him in check. Son of a Black Sea sailor, he had only just finished school before war broke out. Who would have thought then that a few months later he was to be a victim of the nazi murderers?

On October 16, 1941, after 73 days of defence, the Soviet troops had to withdraw from Odessa. As the last Soviet ship put out of the port, the Rumanian and German troops marched into the town.

Captain Vladimir Molodtsov, known then as Badayev, and a group of underground fighters took to the Odessa catacombs. Yasha Gordienko joined Captain Molodtsov's band and acted as a scout. He collected information on the nazis' movements, distributed leaflets and carried on political work among the townspeople. The brave boy often had a hand in the operations—blowing up railway lines, raiding enemy lorries, cutting telephone wires, etc.

Once, due to his initiative and courage, Yasha Gordienko succeeded in rescuing some 50 prisoners.

Yasha was caught in June 1942 at a secret address in Odessa. After taking a traitor in for questioning, agents of the Rumanian political police (sigurantsa) learned the secret addresses of the underground members. It had taken the nazis a long time to catch up with the legendary Badayev. But one evening, when Yasha Gordienko and his commander Badayev were unsuspectingly leaving their hiding-place, the police pounced. Nothing could break their will. The young boy stood up to the torture just as bravely as the experienced Communist Vladimir Molodtsov. They were condemned to death and shot in late July 1942. Yakov Gordienko was posthumously awarded the Order of Lenin and the Partisan of the Patriotic War medal, First Class.

Realising that he was to die in a couple of days, Yasha wrote his last letter home on half a dozen cigarette papers which his cell companions managed to smuggle out to the address indicated.

LETTER
FROM SENIOR LIEUTENANT Y. CHERVONNY

July 1942

Darling Talyushka,

It's hard to begin with common words. When you receive this letter I shall no longer be alive. But there we are, we have to take what comes in life.

Life! The word has such a proud ring. It contains grief and good cheer, suffering and bliss. I'm not going to say life's all the same to me. Not at all, it means a lot. And it's darn hard to lose it.

Youth! What can be dearer than that? I'm not one of the "Dismal Desmonds bearing death with a tirade of curses". No one should play with life. Not to say we shouldn't be afraid of danger. The boys on shore don't have to run so many risks. But I, like so many of my companions, plumped for the sea where there's a greater element of danger and risk. Here a person can really extend himself to the full and do most good. More simply, it was an urge to throw in all I have.

Life can be just a round of daily vegetation like a dumb animal, and life can be free and easy, with wonderful things to look forward to. All of us strive to sling our hammock onto the latter. Our generation has been entrusted with a great and responsible task: to shed our blood and lay down our lives to earn the right to happiness.

I remember when I was a lad at school. My first timid steps when I took my school certificate. The first test—1938-39—

in a prison camp in Spain. That's where I was jolted out of part of the benevolence and habit of seeing everything in a rosy hue, which every young lad and lass does. It was a good lesson in the attempt to understand life. There in Spain I got a fair idea of what we were up against. As a result I decided to devote my whole life to the armed forces, to become an officer. Now you are getting a taste of hatred. It came to me in those days.

Calm and peaceful 1940. A year of stupendous plans for the future. Then came the war. Everyone was faced with the problem of finding his feet and being a worthy son of his country. The old feeling of hatred, the invasion of my beloved Ukraine, losing my father, mother and brother, the realisation that the fight was universal and there was no relying on anyone, aided me right from those early days to decide where I stood and what I was going to do. War came as a test, it put the finishing touches to my character. I gave it all I had. And I can honestly say that nobody can reproach me for any action unworthy of an officer and a Communist.

We were forced to see life in the raw, cruelly and in a much shorter time than age usually allows, but life will be all the dearer to us. Once you know how dear life really is, you don't treat it so lightly as the days go by. I know and am confident that if I'd have got out of this mess in one piece we'd have been so happy together. . . . We live at a time when, before we can lay claim to that happiness, we have to win it in stubborn combat and do our own little bit for the common cause. It makes no difference whether it will be the skill, blood or life. There is no other way.

Remember me now and again as the man who loved you and would lay down his life for his Talyushka without a thought. And that's how it really is. In every common cause there's a part of every man. And for what I gave my part is your cause too. I believed in your love knowing it was crystal clear. It's so wonderful to think of all the times we've had together. . . .

I know it won't be easy for you to get over the idea of losing your Zhenya. But please dear, don't make any foolish pledges. Try to bury all the grief quickly. Try and make your life happy. I'd like to think that in a little while you will forget it all or at least get over it and be happy again. To every man his own fate. There's no getting away from it.

I'd like to say a word of gratitude to your mother, father and little Zoya. They really have looked on me as a son. I wish them a long and happy carefree life. I hope your parents and Zoya will one day have some grandchildren, sons and nieces to nurse and make a fuss of.

One request to you. Once war is over and life gets back to normal try and find my young brother if you can. If he's alive, the country will look after him. He should be a big lad now. Tell him about his Zhenya. Put him on the right lines. His name is Alexander, born in 1930 and left behind in Kherson. I comfort myself that you'll find him. Don't think this is some kind of last wish or an order to look after him. I don't want to burden you with a load of trouble. In our country they look after children and make men out of them. I'm sending you the certificate of my award. Let it be a little souvenir. I don't have anything else.

That's about all. There's so much I want to say, I want to find some tender words to express my feelings. But you know your Zhenya well enough and you understand, don't you, without me writing it down.

Keep your pecker up, look after yourself and put your best foot forward. Be a clever little girl. Don't take it too much to heart. It doesn't help much, you know. Try to make a happy life for yourself and live it for both of us.

Remember your Zhenya now and again, but without any tears and with the thought that he didn't die in vain.

Keep your spirits up,

I love you,

Yevgeny

At the outbreak of war, Senior Lieutenant Yevgeny Chervonny was in Tallinn. In the grim August days of 1941, the torpedo boat on which he served joined up with Soviet ships of the Baltic Fleet leaving Tallinn harbour for Kronstadt. This was a gallant feat of seamanship by the Baltic sailors. Under incessant bombardment, the ships made their way through mine-infested waters to their main base. For his personal bravery and the courageous actions of his crew Yevgeny Chervonny was awarded the Order of the Red Banner.

Yevgeny hated fascism. He had already seen the hate-twisted faces of the bearers of the "New Order". Of a dark August night when there was a lull in the fighting, Yevgeny would look back a few years to 1938 when, a sea cadet at the Kherson Naval School, he had done his navigator's training on the *Skvortsov-Stepanov*, a motor-ship which had been forcibly taken in tow by Franco's men. By starvation and threats, Franco's henchmen had tried to make the Soviet seamen betray their country. They were thrown into stinking holes and left without a drop of water. But most of them came through all these trials. Yevgeny Chervonny returned from prison a sick man. He had contracted T.B. Once home he was cured and became a hardened fighter against fascism. Then came the war. The young officer swore to fight the nazis to his last drop of blood, and to win. These are the selfless and stern lines written by the captain of a section of the 2nd Group of the patrol boats: "He shot down two planes personally. Took part in six mine-laying runs. Had no losses. For 20 days his vessel and a gun-boat supported a section of the coastal army with all its fire.... Took part in three ice runs to Khanko. Saved 400 men...."

One July day in 1942, Senior Lieutenant Chervonny put to sea. It was an operation with practically no chance of coming back alive. Yevgeny knew what he was about. Before putting to sea he wrote his last letter....

His comrades later picked up his body among the debris of the boat that had hit a mine. Yevgeny Chervonny made his final run to Kronstadt wrapped in a naval flag.

In a small yellow case containing his personal effects, his comrades found this letter addressed to his wife.

Yevgeny Chervonny

NOTE FROM
LIEUTENANT LAZAR DZOTOV

August 15, 1942

To my people.

In my service to the Soviet people I'll fight to the last drop of blood for the honour, freedom and independence of Soviet land. I remain true to my war-pledge which I made to my people. To the last minute of my life I count myself a true son of my country.

Forward,

For our country.

Lieutenant Dzotov

Lazar Dzotov, from the North Ossetian village of Dur-Dur, led two platoons of submachine-gunners across a river on the outskirts of Voronezh and silenced enemy gun posts which had prevented Soviet units from making a crossing. This was on August 15, 1942. After being mortally wounded in the battle, he scribbled his last wish down on a piece of paper and passed it on to his comrades.

LETTER
FROM TANK-DRIVER GEORGI LANDAU

Not later than August 20, 1942

Darling, my love,

Yesterday we finally contacted the enemy. Today we'll soon move into the attack.

This is the set-up: artillery and mortars are thundering away, our bombers have just gone over and given Fritz hell.

We are very close to the Germans. All the time nazi mortar shells rend the air and bullets whistle overhead. We're all in good spirits. I'm not the least bit scared, nervous or unsure of myself. Instead, I have a burning love for our country, an urge to do all I can to defend her, my dear ones, from these 20th-century Huns. Get revenge on them for all the misery and suffering they've caused our people, get revenge on them for our beloved Leningrad.

There's a lot more I could write but not much time left.

All my love and kisses to you,
Goga

A war correspondent came upon a tank unit in early August 1942 and got into conversation with the men. Soldiers wanted to recount the battle deeds of their comrades, how life was at the front. There and then the correspondent heard about Lieutenant Landau's letter.

"We used to call him Goga," the tank-men recalled. "He was a fantastically courageous and daring officer. His tank crew were always in front.

"This is his last letter. It was written just before the battle. Goga didn't come back, he died a hero's death. . . ."

NOTE
FROM CADET IVAN SHESTOVSKIKH

August 23, 1942

Today, August 23, we're pounding into the nazi rats. If they kill me, let my country know I died heroically for Stalingrad. I am a candidate to the Party, but please consider me a Party member. Let my country know I died for the cause of the Party.

In July 1942, the nazi forces pushed through to the Volga. Then commenced a battle unprecedented in the history of war, lasting 200 days and nights and culminating in a glorious triumph for the Soviet people.

First into battle and last out were the Communists and Y.C.L. members. The best officers and men joined the Party in those grim days and took the pledge: "Communists won't budge from Stalingrad!" That was the pledge taken by young cadet Ivan Shestovskikh.

NOTE
FROM BATTALION COMMISSAR IVAN SHCHERBINA
TO THE INFANTRY DIVISION COMMAND

September 17-18, 1942

Comrades Kuznetsov and Povarov,

Greetings friends. We're mowing down the Germans surrounding us. Not a step backward—that is my duty and that is my nature. . . .

My regiment hasn't disgraced itself and won't disgrace the Soviet Army.

I sent a letter to a skunk of a German officer. We are hitting you hard and we'll carry on hitting you all the harder.

Comrade Kuznetsov, if I die—my only request is about my family. Another regret is that I can't smash any more of these bastards in the teeth, that is, I'm sorry I have to die so soon with only 85 Gerries to my tally.

For our Soviet Homeland, lads, smash the enemy!

Ivan Shcherbina was born in Dniepropetrovsk in October 12, 1908. On graduating from the Dniepropetrovsk Metallurgical Institute he continued his studies at a Communist Party Institute before serving in the N.K.V.D. (People's Commissariat of Internal Affairs) from 1935. In 1939 he took part in the liberation of Western Ukraine. Just before the war he passed out from the Lenin Military and Political Academy. When war broke out he was appointed Commissar of the 272nd Infantry Regiment. Together with his regiment he made a hard road of retreat to the banks of the Volga.

During the defence of Stalingrad between the 17 and 18 September, 1942, a group of 15-20 soldiers led by a couple of officers defended the Gorky Drama Theatre. Enemy submachine-gunners under the covering fire of tanks broke into the theatre. In order to drive them out again, Ivan Shcherbina and three of his men decided to break through to the main entrance and shoot down the nazis from there. He was the first to dash from cover but was mowed down by a machine-gun burst. The bullets hit him in the neck and shoulder, smashing his carotid artery and his wind-pipe. His strength ebbing away, he managed to jot down a few words to divisional commander, Colonel Kuznetsov, and Colonel Povarov, head of the divisional political department. To his last breath he had faith in the victory of the Soviet people, and with these words fell back in his comrades' arms.

LETTER
FROM GUARDS MAJOR DMITRI PETRAKOV
TO HIS DAUGHTER LUDMILA

September 18, 1942

My little black-eyed Mila,

I'm sending you a cornflower.... Just imagine—the battle's on, enemy shells bursting all around, craters around us and a flower growing here.... And suddenly an explosion ... the cornflower is torn off. I picked it up and put it in my pocket.... The flower had grown, reached for the sun but had been torn off by an explosion, and if I hadn't picked it up it would have been trampled upon. That's how the nazis treat children in the villages they occupy. They murder and trample little children into the ground.... Mila, papa Dima will fight the nazis to his last drop of blood, to his last gasp, so that the nazis won't treat you like this flower. What you don't understand your mama will explain.

Before the war Dmitri Petrakov taught at a college in Ulyanovsk. He was an extremely kind-hearted man. When war broke out he was made educational officer and later regimental commissar.

On September 18, 1942, his battalion attempted to take a hill. Every inch of land had to be gained by furious fighting. For twenty-four hours the battalion soldiers three times warded off counter-attacks. Defying the fire of six-barrelled trench mortars and bombs, the small group edged their way forward. When hand-to-hand fighting ensued, the commissar deliberately ran the risk of calling artillery fire upon his group. He telephoned the artillery and told them to shell the area where he was fighting with his men. Only exceptional gunnery on the part of the Soviet artillery, who wiped out the attacking nazi groups, saved the lives of the heroes. And the hill was taken.

In this encounter Dmitri Petrakov received concussion. When he came to in the medical tent he wrote these few words to his daughter Ludmila, referring to his last battle.

In October 1942, General Gurtyev's Siberian Division in which Dmitri Petrakov was serving clashed with the nazi troops in the factory district of the town. High explosive bombs were crashing all around, walls of buildings came tumbling down and nazi tanks crawled on over the rubble.

Communications were broken. It was then that Major Petrakov led his men into a do-or-die assault on the enemy's rear. The building—the key point of resistance—was captured.

In the summer of the following year, Major Petrakov's regiment began to push towards Orel. The nazis threw all they had into defence, employing more and more Tigers and Panthers. It had to be broken down.

Major Petrakov crawled from trench to trench urging on his officers and men:

"It's only about five miles to Orel. Two or three hours of hard-fought offensive will save us many losses and won't give the Germans a chance to destroy our ancient Russian town. Forward to liberate it!"

These ardent and moving words from their commissar brought a superhuman effort from the soldiers who smashed the enemy's resistance and broke through to the outskirts of the city. Then they pressed on into the streets and squares. But Major Petrakov was dead, killed as he reached the centre of the city.

Dmitri Petrakov

VASILY KRIVOPUSTENKO'S INSCRIPTION IN A NOVOCHERKASSK GESTAPO CELL

September 26, 1942

I slept on this bunk from 24/IX to 26/IX-42, in for interrogation.

They haven't passed sentence but to back up their accusations they confronted me with a stranger, Alexei Yuokhanov.

He gave false testimony and began to lay into me as well, even though he doesn't know me from Adam. Anyway he's a swine and a traitor.

Judging by their attitude at the interrogation and their prejudice I shall be shot.

Farewell. I shall die honourably.

26/IX

V. Krivopustenko

Vasily Krivopustenko was born in Taganrog in 1903 into a poor Don Cossack family. He started work at the age of seven. He became an apprentice to a cobbler, a cowherd and farm labourer.

During the Great October Revolution he joined the Red Guard and then fought for the Red Army against the whiteguards on the Don.

After Civil War he took up work at a shoe factory where he was much admired and respected. For many years he was in charge of deliveries, chairman of his local trade union council, chairman of a district Soviet, instructor at the Party regional committee and, lastly, vice-chairman of the Executive Committee of the Novocherkassk Soviet of Working People's Deputies.

When he went underground with other Communists he organised resistance forces, helped form partisan groups and led raids in the town and on the railway.

While preparing one operation—on September 24, 1942—he was caught by the Gestapo and thrown into a cell.

The Germans knew whom they were dealing with and hardly expected to get anything out of him. So they cruelly beat him up. But he held his tongue. Realising he was doomed he wrote his last lines of farewell to the Soviet people on the plank serving as a cell bed.

FROM A NOTE
WRITTEN BY THREE DEFENDERS OF LISICHANSK

September 28, 1942

... 158th Division ... 259th Regiment. Whoever finds this letter will know that we died for our country. September 28, 1942, in the town of Lisichansk. Seryozha Blinov from Leningrad, 24, wounded Vanya Kharitonov and I, Styopa Mukhin, 26. We swear we shall fight for our country to the end. Please send this to Leningrad, 24 Chapayev Street, District Military Committee. Death to the fascists! Good-bye. We shall die. Avenge us. ...

In the summer of 1960, some boys found an old cartridge case in a ravine near Lisichansk, where the town slopes down to the Northern Donets. There was a small sheet of paper from a school notebook in the cartridge case, on which the vow of the three soldiers had been written in indelible pencil.

The note was in bad shape and it was impossible to make out several words. The surname Blinov was difficult to decipher. It might have been Blitov. But the date September 28, 1942, was fairly clear.

At that time Lisichansk had been a long way behind enemy lines. In July 1942, Hitler's forces had passed farther on to Lugansk and Rostov. In September the fighting had raged up to the Volga. But here is evidence that two and a half months after the fall of Lisichansk fighting was still going on, apparently underground. This trio, like many others, fell defending their native soil, but never surrendered.

LETTERS
FROM NIKOLAI STASHKOV,
SECRETARY OF DNIEPROPETROVSK UNDERGROUND
REGIONAL PARTY COMMITTEE

LETTER TO HIS WIFE, SON AND DAUGHTER

September 26, 1941

Hello there, my little Katenka and Valerik,

Am writing a second letter, today 26-9-41. Staying behind to work. Not afraid and no one made me. If alive we'll meet, and I'll tell you all about it. If not tell the kiddies their dad was no coward and gave his life for Lenin's Party, for his country. Tell them, Katenka, their dad was a real Leninist Bolshevik, remaining to work underground, on a big, responsible job.

If I die be kind to the kids, give them your love. Tell them I expect them to be real patriots of their Soviet land. See they work well at school. . . .

Maybe this is my last letter. Please keep it for memory's sake, for the children.

I want you to know that I loved you all like my dear country. If I die for my country I die for your happiness. Don't blame me, it has to be like that, the circumstances demand it, history demands it and it is people who make history. It fell to me to carry on the fight against these fascist pigs, these beasts, in the underground. We underground fighters will get revenge on the fascist jackals for the blood of fathers, for the destruction and suffering brought on millions of people, for the destruction of my town.

My little darlings, I'm going on a very dangerous mission but I go without any snivelling, for I know that we are in the right, that we shall win sooner or later. Better die a hero than become a slave.

Farewell.

No tears, no grieving. Once more I'm telling you: under the Soviet authorities you won't be left in the lurch, just keep your chin up. . . .

Many, many kisses. Don't write to me,

Dad

LETTER TO HIS COMRADES

September 24, 1942

Comrades,

The prison is riddled with provocateurs. They operate like this: their agent sits with you, tries to pump you. The weaker ones are drawn into conversation. Secrets are given away in gossip. The agent memorises them and passes them on to the interrogator. The next time you come up for interrogation, the same questions are asked. If you don't answer, they give you injections. It's a painful thing to go through. When you come to they tell you that you said this and that under the influence of the pricks. In actual fact it's just the provocateur's notes.

I've had some provocateurs in with me: S. Kulish and Osipenko from Vasilkovsky District and his wife Zina. These three are ex-parachutists but now work for the other side. They've given away over a hundred people. They've had a go at L. Berestov, the Masloprom factory manager, P. Novichuk, my father, V. Bykovsky, Y. Shokhov, N. Tokmakov, Alexander Kravchenko, M. Kalinkin and Yura Savchenko. Osipenko's wife has worked on Vera Khitko, Kharitina Zhuravlyova, Valya Alexeyeva and others.

Farewell comrades!

If you get hold of this note or have a chance to get it out, pass it on or keep it until the Soviet authorities arrive.

Yours,

N. Stashkov

24.IX.42

Nikolai Stashkov, Hero of the
Soviet Union

He returned from the army to his home town of Dniepropetrovsk just two days before the outbreak of war. He had hardly had time to greet his friends and visit his old factory Spartak where he worked many years as a fitter, when the first swastika'd planes appeared over the Dnieper.

Then began frantic days without sleep or rest when he took up work in the Party regional committee. When the enemy came within striking distance of Dniepropetrovsk, Nikolai Stashkov was made secretary of the town underground regional committee of the Party.

The German occupational forces marched into Dniepropetrovsk at the close of August 1941 and began to set up their "New Order" by fire and carnage. Mass arrests of Communists and all Soviet patriots commenced. Between October 13 and 15, the Gestapo and quisling police shot some 12,000 citizens, burying them in an anti-tank trench on the edge of this town. By such fiendish actions the nazis wanted to coerce the Soviet people, to bring them to their knees.

From day to day the partisan and underground movement steadily grew under the guidance of the Party's underground regional committee. Between October and November 1941, Nikolai Stashkov went on foot round many districts and established personal contacts with the leaders of Pavlograd, Sinelnikovo and other underground town and district Party committees. He also made contact with leaders of Y.C.L. organisations. In November he held a "forest" Party conference attended by Communists from partisan detachments in the region. In January and April of the following year, he was responsible for meetings in Pavlograd of secretaries of underground town and district Party committees.

The workers of Dniepropetrovsk and Dnieprodzerzhinsk, the miners of Krivorozhye and Marganets, the working men of other industrial centres frustrated a good many enemy plans. The nazis were given no peace anywhere and the ground everywhere burned under their feet. They were never able to get any sizable factory going. Their ruined tanks, guns, train engines and lorries had to be sent to Germany for repairs. Railway blasts grew, smashing carriages with troops and equipment.

The Gestapo had their work cut out searching high and low for the people behind the resistance. In the end, one of their spies managed to attend the "wedding" of a young underground pair,

Vera Khitko and Nikolai Tokmakov, which was in fact a cover for Stashkov to brief his men. This was in June 1942.

After the "wedding" came the first round of arrests. This was followed on July 8-9 by the second and more damaging arrests. Yet the Gestapo could not pin down the leader. At the beginning of July, Nikolai Stashkov made his way to Pavlograd where the underground Party regional committee had its base. He now directed operations from there.

Trouble came unexpected. On July 28, he was wandering through the town market on his way to a rendezvous with some contacts. He was trailed by a spy who suddenly shot him in the thigh and arm. Wounded, he had little chance of escape and was caught by the Gestapo quickly hurrying onto the scene.

Head of the local S.D. Sturmbanführer Muhlde rushed to Pavlograd and took the prisoner away under heavy guard to Dniepropetrovsk. He was put into cell No. 20 of the Gestapo prison in Korolenko Street.

Even before his wounds had healed he was constantly badgered by high-ranking officers of the Gestapo and nazi administration. The nazis did their level best to make him change sides. When they saw it was useless they devised hideous torture for the brave Communist and then planted a provocateur in his cell. During this time Nikolai Stashkov discovered they had not even spared his 75-year-old father and had shot him in front of the townspeople.

Yet even in prison, the underground leader felt himself responsible for the fate of his comrades and did all he could to cheer them up. This is evident from the letter to his comrades printed above.

On December 10, 1942, the prisoners saw some of their comrades being taken out before the firing squad.

"Farewell, comrades!" called out Nikolai Stashkov.

A few weeks later, Nikolai Stashkov and his faithful companion Georgi Savchenko were led out to face the firing squad. Stashkov shouted out to the butchers: "Shoot me in the chest. I know you haven't got the guts. You'll shoot me in the back of the head. You're even afraid of the dead!"

For his bravery in war Nikolai Stashkov was posthumously awarded the title of the Hero of the Soviet Union and had one of the streets of Dniepropetrovsk named after him.

NOTE
FROM THREE SOVIET GIRL-SCOUTS
FROM A GESTAPO GAOL IN PSKOV

October 17, 1942

Today is October 17, 1942. More than a month we've been in this cell. Three of us. We have done our duty to our country honourably. For that the nazis are torturing us. No matter what they do we'll die honourably as in battle. Farewell, comrades! Revenge us.

This short note on a page of a school exercise-book was discovered in 1957 by some builders behind a door-frame in one of the cells of the former Gestapo gaol in Pskov. On one side of the paper was the outline of the red banner traced in blood and on the other the above words.

The story behind the note is as follows.

On the night of August 8, 1942, four young girls were dropped by parachute behind enemy lines near Pskov. The quartette, under the code name *Vera*, consisted of Valeria Patkovskaya, 20, Valentina Golubeva, 19, Yelena Silanova, 18, and Anfisa Gorbunova, 23. All the girls were from Moscow. Their instructions were to settle down in Pskov and radio information on the location of enemy troops, their movements and strength, the defence fortifications, etc., to the Soviet Army H.Q. After a safe landing, the girls had the misfortune of running into a search party the next day somewhere near Zarechye. Three escaped but Yelena Silanova lost her life in the shooting.

From a house on the outskirts of Pskov the trio started their regular transmission of ciphers back to headquarters, keeping watch on the junctions of all the main highways leading out of Pskov. At the end of August they were forced to leave their convenient room because the old landlord had been arrested and tortured to death by the Gestapo. After registering at the Labour Exchange they quickly found jobs: Valentina (under the name of Izotova) and Anfisa (under the name of Mazina) at a cord factory, and Valeria (under the name of Shchedrova) as an interpreter in a German office.

In September, during a registration check on Soviet citizens, they were all summoned to the commandatura and detained because of some irregularity with their passports. Initially, as there was no evidence against the girls, they were held in Abwehrkommand No. 304 on Krestyanskaya Street where the police were checking all suspects and their papers, besides recruiting people. The conditions were a good deal more free and easy than in gaol and the girls got ready to make a break. But suddenly everything fell through. A woman was brought to the Abwehrkommand who knew Valeria well. During questioning she blurted out Valeria's real surname and, unable to withstand the torture, gave her away as the leader of the intelligence group. The next day Valeria Patkovskaya and her two companions were carted off to the Gestapo gaol.

There the girls were strung up, burnt with flaming torches and clubbed mercilessly. Then the nazis took the brave trio beyond the town to the village of Peski and shot them.

LETTERS FROM KONSTANTIN ZASLONOV, COMMANDER OF ORSHA PARTISAN BRIGADE

LETTER TO A FRIEND

Not later than November 14, 1942

My dear Vladimir Yakovlevich,

Best partisan greetings from the dense thickets, swamps, woods and partisan hamlets of Byelorussia.

When old pals meet they usually ask each other, "Well, how're things going?" That's probably the question you'd like to put to me. The usual reply is "Fair enough". Then we can get on with our chat as friends and comrades do. It's a year since we parted, a year knocking around different parts, sometimes envying each other.... I know it, we'd get chatting as if we had only seen each other yesterday, I can just imagine it. First of all, I'll begin with what interests you just as keenly as other affairs of state—your only son.... The boy lives in Slavny with your brother-in-law. Your dear mother-in-law has been there too ever since her home was bombed last February.

Now to business. Big things—we blast, blast and blast again. Every day something new, sometimes we hack away—no mercy to the Germans, sometimes it suits us better to lie low and sometimes we watch the nazis bite the dust from a derailed train. Sometimes we eat like kings, sleep like logs, sometimes we go hungry for five days, sometimes we're chilled to the marrow and our teeth chatter. There are provocateurs about, spies and traitors around, sometimes we let them slip through our fingers but more often they taste the vengeance

My partisans got the Gerries so worked up they had to muster and throw in three divisions against me but we made it so hot for them they cleared off. Now the price on my head has gone up and gets even higher after every sortie, and sorties come thick and fast. Now the price on my head is 50,000 marks, an Iron Cross and, into the bargain, whoever delivers me dead or alive to the German authorities, will be granted a wonderful life in Germany with all his relatives. If any of the peasants give me away to the authorities they'll be given two large German estates for their own use for life.

There we are, Vladimir Yakovlevich, that's about the size of it.

I must admit, along with my men's heroism and bravery there are the cowards and quislings. We've learned how to deal with such people and we're doing alright, erasing them from our life like one of nature's errors. Details of our skirmishes and forays when we meet. I've just about walked my feet off covering the length and breadth of Byelorussia, although sometimes we get a lift.

Well, Volodya, all the best. Greetings, Zaslonov.

Greetings to the boys on the railway, see if you can scrape together a decent group of about 15-20 men and pay us a call for a couple of months, we'll have a few scraps and you can fly back again. Come and be my guest with the boys, you can contact me through Comrade Ponomarenko, he knows where I am.

Zaslonov

LETTER HOME

Not later than November 14, 1942

My dear little Ritusya, my darling pets Muza and Iza. How much I'd love to see you all. If we pull through we'll be together again. If I die, it's for our country. That's how to put it to the kiddies. . . .

With a heavy heart Konstantin Zaslonov left Orsha on July 15, 1941. He caught the last train for the east literally right under the noses of the German motorcyclists. It was a hard trip to Moscow. Finally, he reached the blacked-out, austere capital at the Ilyich rail-

Konstantin Zaslonov, Hero of the
Soviet Union

way shed on the Byelorussian line. There were several railwaymen from Orsha already at work there and Konstantin Zaslonov was put in charge of the repaired engines. One day he gathered his friends about him and read out an appeal to the Party Central Committee and the Ministry of Transport:

"Our country is in flames. Life demands that every citizen with the heart of a patriot stand up to defend our country.... I beg your permission to form a partisan detachment and operate between Yartsevo and Baranovichi, including the strip of railway line, stations and other railway installations. I assure you in the name of the bravest of our lads who have asked me to appeal to you, that we swear to keep the partisan oath with honour...."

This appeal expressed the thoughts and hopes of all present, and soon afterwards some 30 Orsha and Smolensk railwaymen were getting ready for their trip behind the lines. Zaslonov was appointed commander with F. Yakushev as his commissar. In early September the small partisan group set out for Vyazma where they were joined by another group of workers.

At dawn on October 1, 1941, Zaslonov's men crossed the front near Belsk, assisted by the covering fire of a squadron of the Major-General Dovator's cavalry corps. The partisans slogged it out for one and a half months surmounting all possible hazards, bearing all the privations of early winter, giving many German search parties the slip and suffering from cold and hunger.

Only a few reached Orsha.... In the town, Konstantin Zaslonov soon made contact with the Communists left behind for underground work in the enemy rear. With their assistance he managed to get from the town authorities a temporary pass and then was allowed to sign on for work at the Labour Exchange.

The jobless engineer, born in 1909, and having worked in the local railway depot for a long time before the war, quickly attracted the attention of the German administration who were badly in need of specialists to set things right on the railway. After careful checks, the "loyal" engineer was put in charge of Russian engine crews.

Making use of his position, Konstantin Zaslonov was able to fix up work for his companions from Vyazma—Anatoly Andreyev, Sergei Chebrikov and Pyotr Shurmin. This tiny group acted as the nucleus of the resistance movement and carried on all manner of diversions in Orsha and at neighbouring railway stations. Many railway workers joined the resistance.

NOTE
FROM SEVENTEEN BYELORUSSIAN PARTISANS

December 3, 1942

We die for our country, but shall not let the enemy through.
Please consider us all Komsomol members.

It was the second rigorous winter of the war. The nazi invaders had occupied Byelorussia and subjected her people to unprecedented suffering. But the Byelorussian people refused to bow down to the fascist butchers. A mighty partisan movement sprang up throughout the occupied territory.

A group of 17 young Byelorussian partisans led by Communist Vikenty Drozdovich was active in the Kopyl District.

On December 3, 1942, this small group of men received an order from brigade headquarters to stop the nazis moving towards the village of Lava, location of a partisan hospital and the brigade headquarters. For four hours the brave seventeen youngsters beat off eight enemy attacks backed by light tanks, armoured cars, artillery and mortar fire.

The Soviet patriots made a pledge to their country they would fight off the enemy until their last gasp. When their ammunition and hand grenades ran out, they continued with rifle butts and bayonets. A total of 85 Germans were killed and several light tanks and armoured cars put out of action.

In the grossly unequal battle on December 3, 1942, all 17 patriots fell. At the cost of their lives the heroes had given their people a breathing space to evacuate the hospital and assemble their forces for combat. The partisan brigade routed the Germans who had to pay dearly with hundreds of lives for the death of the gallant seventeen.

Despite the hard conditions under which they operated, the incessant Gestapo checks and spying by German agents, Zaslonov and his comrades trained the repair workers in subversive tactics and skill. The group made their own mines disguised as lumps of coal which they hid under coal heaps. They also made "hedgehogs"—special explosives which were scattered along the highways. The resistance men blew up signal boxes, pump-houses, railway points and bridges, burned down buildings and killed enemy soldiers and officers.

From Zaslonov's dispatches to the Vitebsk Party underground committee it is seen that in three months of the heroic campaign at Orsha railway junction there were 98 train crashes, 200 locomotives were knocked out and thousands of waggons and fuel cisterns and large quantities of enemy equipment were blown up. This was a tremendous help to the Soviet Army fighting the Germans near Moscow.

Besides, Zaslonov's men seized arms and built up a store to move out to the forest. On several occasions the German administration arrested Zaslonov, but every time he was able to establish his non-implication in sabotage. But in February 1942, when it had become too dangerous to remain at the shed any longer Zaslonov and his companions left for the south-west of Vitebsk Region leaving behind a few trusted people on the railway. At the new base, the village of Logi, a detachment named "Uncle Kostya" began to function. It quickly grew. By June it had notched up 113 blown-up trains and some 2,000 dead nazis and quislings. Soon after, the five detachments were united in the 2,500-strong Zaslonov brigade.

Between October and November the partisans caused a great deal of discomfort to the better-equipped and more numerous nazis based on Vitebsk. On November 13, the Germans succeeded in surrounding a group of commanders and commissars of the Orsha zone partisan detachments who had gathered for a conflab in the village of Kupovat. On the following morning the Germans closed in. After four hours of furious fighting the enemy broke through to the edge of the village. Hand-to-hand combat commenced. All the partisans and their officers fought to their last cartridge, to their last gasp.

He perished. But other partisan brigades bore his name and courageously fulfilled the deeds of one of the Soviet Union's bravest sons.

LETTER AND NOTES
FROM GEORGI SAVCHENKO, LEADER
OF DNIEPROPETROVSK UNDERGROUND

LETTER HOME

Dear Mum and Dad and sister Tina,

If we ever meet again—and even though things are pretty tough now I don't lose hope—I'll let you know a little more. For the time being I'm just writing a few words about what has happened to me in the past nine or ten months. This period in my life is a darn sight richer in experience than all the other years put together. In this time I've had to go through just about the lot—starting from my baptism of fire and ending with concentration camps. So I've seen quite a bit.

Up to August we retreated, fighting, eastwards. Then our unit was surrounded and this is where things started. P.o.w. camp. Escape. A few days of freedom. Inside again. Out again. And inside again. This time I'm locked in the Bobruisk Fortress. They started to beat the living daylights out of me, after which I was about a fortnight on my back. I'd only just got over it when I had another go at getting out. I thought I'd make for Dniepropetrovsk to see you all and get back into the fray.

Why am I doing all this?

1) I'm a Communist. Not just in words but after going through an extensive communist school. My Party card is my whole life to me, not a screen behind which one can hide from life's tempests at the first moment of trial.

2) All the things I've been through force me to this decision. I grew up, studied and matured in Soviet times. That has

entered my blood and flesh. To live without or outside the Soviet system is simply unthinkable for me. I'll fight might and mane to see the red flag flying again over our country and our Dniepropetrovsk and to get the country free of these gorillas, these bandits, these bloodsuckers. . . .

Hatred makes my blood boil. No swine of a nazi I get my hands on will escape with his life. Death to the bastards who have besmirched our sacred land!

If I don't come back you will know I gave everything to liberate my country, I died for you, my dear ones.

I hope it is only "good-bye till we meet again".

Lots of kisses,

Your loving son and brother,

Yuri

March 19, 1942
Dniepropetrovsk

NOTE TO HIS AUNT K. A. SHEPITKO

Thanks for the bread and especially for the linen. Auntie dear. I'm so sorry I've caused you and everyone at home so much sorrow. It doesn't look as if I'll get out of here. We are all due to be shot today or tomorrow. But I've no regrets. We shall win all the same. Tell Klava to bring up Galya a decent and honest girl. She'll have a hard time without her husband, and so will the little girl without her dad. Let's hope she marries again if she finds a suitable chap. I lay down my life for my country.

Farewell.

NOTE TO HIS COMPANIONS

Greetings friends,

Thanks for all you've done for me. This note looks like being my last "will and testament".

The case is already over and I'll be pushing up the daisies today or tomorrow.

If you can get to see my folks, give them a kiss for me.

Yours,

Yuri

Once more please excuse the bother I've caused. I'd give anything to live. But I'll go calmly in the knowledge that I'm not the only one and there will be thousands of others who'll take my place.

P.S. Wash out my linen and pass it on in a separate bundle. Don't bring anything else.

December 21, 1942

Up to the war Georgi Savchenko was an electrical fitter at the Petrovsky Works in Dniepropetrovsk. In 1939, he joined up, went through a military-political college and became a political instructor. In July 1941, his unit was encircled. In an attempt to break through to his own men he was taken prisoner. Thrice he made a break from captivity. Twice he was caught but the third time he managed to get back to his native town where, together with a group of youngsters, he formed a Party resistance group. At the beginning of February 1941, the organisation numbered more than a hundred.

In a dark and dimly-lit cellar the resistance fighters rigged up a transmitter and began to listen in to the voice of Moscow. They jotted down the news, wrote out leaflets and distributed them around the town. The leaflets were signed simply: Committee C.P.(B.)U.—(Communist Party [Bolsheviks] of the Ukraine).

At the outset to 1942, the Germans decided to set the town's biggest factories in motion—including the Petrovsky, the Artyom and several

Georgi Savchenko

others. The resistance men and women intended to do all they could to foil the Germans' plans. At the Petrovsky Plant an underground group was set up to sabotage operations. Once they managed to destroy the valuable cable which had arrived to the works. In the end, the Germans had to give up their idea of trying to make the factories work.

In the spring of 1942, Savchenko was elected secretary of the underground town Party committee. Groups of young resistance fighters sprang up and established contact with the neighbouring settlements. The participants in the organisation worked out a plan for an uprising in the town and collected arms and ammunition in preparation. They blew up a gun-powder store, a fuel dump in Nizhnednieprovsk, and a number of other targets. They destroyed trains, lorries and killed German soldiers.

Despite the desperate efforts of the Gestapo the underground remained a mystery to the Germans for some time. Finally, a spy succeeded in worming his way into one of the groups.

The round-up commenced. In just one week more than 70 people were brought in.

Georgi Savchenko managed to escape several times from under the very noses of the Gestapo, until he was finally arrested in October 1942 when, scorning danger, he was putting the resistance back on its feet. In early December the nazis shot a large group of resistance fighters on the outskirts of the town. Savchenko faced the firing squad at the end of January 1943 together with Nikolai Stashkov, secretary of the underground Party regional committee.

Georgi Savchenko's letter was discovered in his old apartment on Krasnoflotskaya Lane. It was hidden behind the frame of a picture hanging next to a family portrait. He also managed to have two notes smuggled out of gaol. The first was to his aunt who was let out of prison shortly before his arrest. She persuaded the prison guard to pass on to her nephew a loaf of bread and a change of linen. An hour later the guard brought back the note hastily scribbled on a scrap of paper. The second note was smuggled out on a piece of cloth shortly before his execution.

LETTERS
FROM MINSK RESISTANCE FIGHTERS
IVAN KOZLOV AND GEORGI FALEVICH

LETTER FROM IVAN KOZLOV TO HIS COMRADES

December 27, 1942

My dears,

Yesterday, Saturday, I received no correspondence from you. Understood. I'll probably be the death of you with my straightforwardness but there's no sense giving way to despair when there's no way of mending what's done. Everything I've got worked out, as you see, cannot be realised for reasons which are beyond my control. I know it must be hard to lose one of your mates. But how can you help? Tears are no use. To hell with them. Millions are dying and in what way are we better than them? A real patriot is who looks death bravely in the face. No tears. No despair. Our blood won't be shed in vain.

Have courage, be brave, don't be afraid and never despair.

What wouldn't I give to live and get revenge on these savages! If only I were able.... You can bet your life I would have slaughtered these dirty swine. I wouldn't have cared, I would have torn them apart—and enjoyed every minute of it. Yet only a couple of years ago I was too scared even to carve a little chicken.

Oh, how I want to live! The whole aim of life is not to hide behind the backs of your comrades but to take a gun in your hands and kill the dirty jackals. The whole ecstasy of life, the eternal ideal of us all is to live for our country, for our freedom-loving Russian nation, to battle for its honour and freedom.

Ardent greetings to all those who go with gun in hands to defend honour and independence.

Greetings to all friends and comrades. . . .

From the very bottom of my heart I wish you the best of luck. Please excuse the torments I'm causing you, they'll be paid back in full.

Yours,
Vanya Kozlov

See if you can get me a bit of baccy today round about three.

GEORGI FALEVICH'S LETTER TO HIS FIANCÉE

Not later than September 1942

My love, what a pity I can't write to you from here, I'd swamp you with letters.

My darling, how I want to see you, kiss you and hold you in my arms. But, unfortunately, all that is impossible both now and in the future. Nina dear, please try and slip me a few words somehow. My love, write me something every day. It would make me so happy. . . .

Give mum a kiss for me. Ask Vera Ignatyevna to forgive me for everything—kiss her too.

I could do with a smoke!

All my love,
Georgi

Tell them at home there is a note sewn in my underpants.

On June 28, 1941, the nazis marched into Minsk, but they were unable to break its people's spirit. In the very first months of occupation the Communists and Y.C.L. members began to get together small resistance groups at the big factories, on the railway and in the colleges. At the end of 1941 a town Party committee came into being to lead the resistance struggle. Set up at the same time was a Military Council of Partisan Detachments consisting mainly of soldiers and officers who had stayed behind in the Byelorussian capital.

One of their first tasks was to listen in to the news from Moscow and to distribute leaflets. After establishing contact with the partisans, the underground resistance began to engage in intelligence work and supply the partisans with arms and ammunition, medicine and warm clothing. In order to carry out intelligence work more efficiently the Minsk patriots, on instructions from the Party committee, made their way into jobs at offices and factories run by the Germans.

Ivan Kozlov was one of the most active of the Minsk underground workers. Right from the very first days of occupation Kozlov turned his house into a meeting place for his fellow resistance fighters, intelligence people and partisans. He handled

Ivan Kozlov

all the messages which the partisans sent to the underground and back again. On instructions from the Party committee, he became engaged on the job of preparing documents for the underground. In the squat house on Komarovskaya Street this talented artist forged the stamps and signatures of the nazi administrators in Minsk. He was supplied with blank documents by another member of the underground, Y.C.L. lad Zakhar Gallo who got himself a job as clerk in the German pass office. Risking his life daily Gallo brought Kozlov blank passports, passes and other documents, specimens of stamps and signatures. The pair of them supplied dozens of Minsk fighters with life-saving documents. It took the Germans a long time before they could lay their hands on the underground pass-issuing office.

Between September and October 1942, the Gestapo, with the connivance of spies who had wormed their way into the Minsk underground, dealt a serious blow to the Party organisation. On October 26, Kozlov was arrested. More than two months of endless questioning and torture went by. Nothing could break the will of the intrepid Soviet patriot. Not one name passed his lips.

His friends prepared an escape plan, but it fell through at the last moment.

From time to time Ivan Kozlov succeeded in making contact with his friends outside continuing the fight against the enemy. On December 27, 1942, not long before his execution, he wrote them the letter published above. His last words found their way through to his comrades-in-arms and from them were sent to the partisans.

* * *

105

Georgi Falevich had been a chemistry student at the Byelorussia State University. He could hardly have imagined that in a few months' time he was to be in charge of a dispensary under the Germans. But the underground needed a reliable cover and they needed medical supplies, and the chemistry undergraduate took over a dispensary on Sovietskaya St. right next door to the Gestapo H.Q. Another undergraduate, Nina Yermolenko, joined her fiancé at the dispensary.

All autumn and winter of 1941-42, the dispensary manager's office served as a reliable cover for the partisans. Here they kept their print and blank bread coupons with which they supplied the underground fighters and partisan families. And a good deal of scarce medical supplies were dispatched from here to the partisan units.

In the spring of 1942, a spy succeeded in penetrating the organisation. Arrests commenced. On the morning of May 26, the Gestapo pounced on two girls—partisan contacts—with whom Georgi Falevich had sent an urgent order of medical supplies for the partisans. The dispensary was cordoned off and all its assistants put under arrest. Due to lack of evidence Nina Yermolenko was quickly released but Georgi Falevich and his comrades were taken away to the town Gestapo gaol.

The nazis tried every trick they knew to get information out of the young chemist. But they got no names or addresses. The young lad stood up to his torture bravely and took all blame on himself in an effort to save the remaining underground fighters under arrest. In September the Germans stopped taking any more parcels from Nina for Georgi. It was later learned that he had been shot.

Through a policeman in league with the underground, Georgi Falevich managed to send out a few letters to his bride-to-be. They were written on narrow strips of cloth torn from his clothing.

INSCRIPTIONS
ON THE WALLS OF PRISON BARRACKS
IN CHISTYAKOVO, DONBAS

Late 1942

Brothers! Black Sea sailors,
Don't think I was taken prisoner for nothing. I was gravely wounded but these dirty bastards patched me up to use me as their workhorse. No go. Today they set on me, broke just about every bone in my body, farewell.

Yours, Mikhail L.

I'll be gone today but you'll stay behind, Black Sea sailors. Fire a few rounds for me, brothers, let'em know we won't give in, that I'm gone but you remain.

Yours, Nikolai G.

Farewell to all my dear ones. How I'd like to get just one more look at my sea, my Black Sea.

P. T.

Kid brother, Kolya, dear sailor boy,
Remember me, look after mum.

Your brother Oleg

After the fall of Odessa and Sevastopol, a group of Black Sea sailors were taken prisoner and enclosed in the Chistyakovo prison barracks, in the Donbas. According to eye-witness reports the seamen were treated in an abominable way. In a note concealed in a stove in one of the barracks, a tank man wrote: "They were tortured, branded with white-hot irons, had their hands twisted off, and they said: 'Listen, friends, if anyone succeeds in getting out of here alive, don't forget to tell everyone that sailors are made of steel and no force on earth can drive us down. Long live our country! Long live our Ukraine!'

"These are the words spoken by the sailors under torture, and they were tortured before the eyes of all us prisoners so as to break down our resistance. We later learned that the sailors had strangled two German guards, but they didn't manage to escape...."

Unfortunately, the names of the Black Sea heroes have not yet been established.

NOTE
FROM NIKOLAI BUKIN, ONE OF THE KHERSON UNDERGROUND LEADERS

Early 1943

Even if they tear me to pieces, they won't get anything from me!

Nikolai Bukin hailed from the Soviet Far North, the settlement of Nivsk in Kandalaksha District. After crowning an excellent school career in 1939, he volunteered for the army.

As soon as war began he was right in the thick of the fighting. In a letter home sent on September 16, 1941, he wrote: "Now we have to fight and fight to the death, for to die in battle is an honour, to live in slavery is a sin.... I go to my death like all those who defend every inch of Soviet soil from the swine who strive to enslave and destroy our fathers, mothers, sisters and brothers...."

While defending the lower reaches of the Dnieper, the young soldier was seriously wounded and taken prisoner. But not for long. He escaped and made contact with the Y.C.L. members of Kherson and, together with Ilya Kulik, headed the young underground fighters. The patriots derailed enemy trains, stuck up leaflets in the streets of the town and assassinated nazis.

One day the Gestapo tracked Nikolai Bukin down and tried to take him alive. "To die in battle is an honour," was the young man's motto. And he

Nikolai Bukin

saved his last bullet for himself. He regained consciousness in a condemned cell. The Gestapo nursed him back to health in order to squeeze the names of other underground fighters from him. But he didn't lose heart and was constantly trying to keep his neighbours' spirits up. He managed to communicate to them his last, courageous letter.

A survivor of the Kherson underground, Klava Shapovalova, wrote to Nikolai Bukin's parents about the last days of their son's life: "I remember seeing him one day.... And you know, no matter how brutally they battered him, I never once saw a spark of fear of death in his eyes. People like Nikolai don't cry. That's how he will always remain in my memory...."

NINA POPTSOVA'S LETTER
FROM PYATIGORSK GESTAPO DUNGEON

January 6, 1943

Farewell Mummy. I'll soon be gone. Don't cry over me.

Mum, when our Red Army comes, let them know I died for my country. Let them avenge me and our suffering.

My dear Mum, farewell once more ... we shan't be seeing each other any more. I'm going to die.

But how much I want to live! I'm only 20, and death is knocking at the door....

How much I want to work, to serve my country.

But these savages, murderers.... They snatch our young lives away.

I'm now in the death cell, waiting for them to come along at any moment. I can hear them shouting "Come out!", they're coming to the cell now....

Oh, Mum, farewell! Kisses to you all for the last time. My final greetings and kisses....

Nina Poptsova

Nina Poptsova was a twenty-year-old Y.C.L. girl from a little hamlet near Pyatigorsk. At the approach of Hitler's army she took to the hills to fight the enemy from there. In late autumn 1942, she was dropped by parachute behind the front line to glean what information she could about the nazi troops. On instructions from her command, Nina made three excursions behind the lines. On one occasion she got through to Pyatigorsk, and on another to her native village; she even fearlessly entered nazi offices. And everywhere her sharp eyes took in exactly what was needed back at command headquarters.

Nina twice safely crossed the front and delivered her information to headquarters. When she appeared for the third time in the streets of Pyatigorsk she was spotted by a traitor and given away to the Germans. In the Pyatigorsk dungeons she was interrogated by officers from the notorious Bergman Regiment with the participation of the fascist butcher Oberländer. But they were unable to force a word from the young girl. On the day of her death, January 6, 1943, five days before Pyatigorsk's liberation, Nina wrote a letter to her mother. This letter, hurriedly scribbled in pencil, was discovered among the documents left behind by the Germans in their hurried exit from the town.

LIDIA BELOVA'S LETTER
FROM NIKOPOL PRISON

Not later than January 7, 1943*

My dearest Papa, Mama, dear sister Nyura and my darling son,

Thanks a lot for the two notes. I'm very pleased to have heard your dear voice.

We haven't got any idea yet what they are going to do with us—either camp or the shooting squad. It's all the same to us whether we live like that or die. There are many of us here who were arrested on political grounds. And none of us is in low spirits ... talking and thinking about the future, and not giving death a thought. Papa, it's better to die on our own soil than be taken to Germany.

I'm not scared of dying, I'm just a bit sorry for you and my son. Still, let's not think of death, let's think of the future.

Best wishes to you all. . . .

Lots of love,
Lidia

Lidia Belova was a member of Nikifor Taraskin's underground group of young people in the village of Alexeyevka, in Zaporozhye Region.

Their chief mission was to carry out agitation among the population. Under Taraskin's guidance, several brave girls, including Belova, wrote out leaflets and appeals to the local population urging them to combat the measures taken by the occupational forces, in particular the dispatch of young people to Germany. They urged the people to destroy farm produce deliveries and disrupt enemy transport. These leaflets were posted all over the district

* Date she was shot.

Due to the inexperience of certain members of the organisation, the group was uncovered after it had been operating for over four months. At the end of November 1942, Taraskin was taken in along with other members. The arrested were detained in Nikopol prison until January 1943, from where they succeeded in sending several letters home.

Neither the brutal interrogations, nor the torture, nor imminent death could break Lidia's will or that of her wonderful companions.

On the morning of January 7, 1943, the nazis led the Komsomol girls out to be shot. They were taken by car to the edge of the town. When the car was drawing near their place of execution, the girls, at a sign from Taraskin, threw themselves on their guards, disarmed them, threw them out of the car and jumped down themselves. But the soldiers following in another car mowed them down with a burst of machine-gun fire.

NOTES AND INSCRIPTIONS
MADE ON THE WALLS OF PRISON CELLS
BY MEMBERS OF THE YOUNG GUARD

Not later than February 9, 1943

INSCRIPTIONS ON A CELL WALL IN KRASNODON

Captured Gukov V. S. 6.1.43.
Bondareva, Minayeva, Gromova and Samoshina.
Murdered by nazis 15/1/43, 9 p.m.
Death to the German invaders!

NOTE FROM MARIA DYMCHENKO

Dear sisters,

No hope of returning home. Due to be shot, pity on the kiddies. Look after my children. It'll be tough for them without a mother and father. I haven't lost hope and I know the Soviet authorities will bring them up as they did me. Our men will soon be back. We shall fight to the end....

Long to live. Look after yourselves,

January 14, 1943

Maria

NOTE LEFT BY KLAVA KOVALYOVA

Dear Mummy,

If dad survives let him get . . .* for me—as the saying goes: "An eye for an eye, a tooth for a tooth."

I won't be coming home, hide my diary.

Greetings

January 14, 1943

Klava

---

* Names of policemen are omitted.

IVAN ZEMNUKHOV'S INSCRIPTION

Not later than January 15, 1943*

Dear Mum and Dad,

It all has to be endured somehow. Love from your loving son,

Zemnukhov

LYUBOV SHEVTSOVA'S NOTES

January 1943

Greetings dear Mama and Mikhailovna,

Now you know where I am, Mum. . . . Please pardon me for all I've done, perhaps I'll see you for the last time but I don't suppose I'll ever see dad again.

Mama, please give my regards to Auntie Masha and all the others. Don't take it too much to heart, for the time being good-bye.

Yours,
Lyubasha

Not later than February 9, 1943**

Farewell, Mama, your daughter Lyuba is going into the damp earth.

LYUBOV SHEVTSOVA'S INSCRIPTIONS

February 7, 1943

I'm thinking of you at this moment, Mama,

Your Lyubasha

Please forgive me. They've taken me forever.

Shevtsova

---

* Ivan Zemnukhov was killed on the night of January 15, 1943.
** Lyubov Shevtsova was shot on February 9, 1943.

116

Even before the occupation of Krasnodon, the Lugansk Regional Party Committee set about organising a Bolshevik underground. Philip Lyutikov, Party member since 1924, was put in charge of the Krasnodon organisation. On July 20, 1942, the nazis marched into Karsnodon and mass arrests began. Many of the resistance fighters were rounded up and shot, but the nazis failed to smash the underground completely. Lyutikov and other Communists did what they could to patch up contacts with the remaining Y.C.L. members in the town. Y.C.L. underground groups began to spring up. Organisation in the centre of the town was run by Ivan Zemnukhov and Oleg Koshevoi, one of the outlying districts by Sergei Tyulenin, the settlement Pervomaika by Anatoly Popov, Ulyana Gromova and Maya Peglivanova, the Krasnodon settlement by Nikolai Sumskoj and Antonina Yeliseyenko, the village of Novo-Alexandrovka by Klava Kovalyova and the village of Sheverevka by Stepan Safonov.

Ivan Zemnukhov, Hero of the Soviet Union

At the end of September 1942, the first organised meeting of the young underground fighters took place at which they set up an H.A. under the name The Young Guard,* at the suggestion of Sergei Tyulenin. In early October, after the unification of all the underground groups, Shevtsova and Gromova joined Turkenich, Tretyakevich, Zemnukhov, Koshevoi, Tyulenin and Levashov at the H.Q. Oleg Koshevoi was made secretary of the underground Y.C.L. organisation, Victor Tretyakevich was put in charge of organisational work and Ivan Turkenich was put in charge of operations. By the end of October the Krasnodon underground organisation numbered over 100 members broken down into groups of five.

The Young Guard brought the local people news from the front and behind Soviet lines. During the occupation they produced more than 30 kinds of leaflets in a total of 5,000-odd copies. They sabotaged farm supplies deliveries to the Germans, blew up stores and ruined mine equipment. They organised the escape of 20 p.o.w.s from the Pervomaisk hospital and more than 70 from the camp in Volchansk village. On December 5, on Soviet Constitution Day, they burned down

---

* The book *The Young Guard* by Fadeyev, translated into English by Progress Publishers, gives a detailed account of the young people's heroic activities.

Lyubov Shevtsova, Hero of the
Soviet Union

the German Labour Exchange, thus rescuing several thousand Soviet people from being shipped to work in Germany. The Young Guard was preparing for an armed uprising the moment Soviet Army units drew near.

Their downfall came unexpectedly. On the morning of January 1, 1943, the police arrested Moshkov and Tretyakevich. As soon as he put in an appearance at the police station to clear his companions, Zemnukhov, too, was taken in custody.

The daring Y.C.L. members were given away by Gennady Pocheptsov who was egged on by his step-father. When he learned of the arrest of the three this cowardly traitor, wanting to curry favour with the Germans, supplied the names of many of the other Young Guards.

First to be rounded up were the entire 18 members of the Pervomaika underground. Simultaneously, arrests began in the town. Four cells of the town police station were filled to overflowing. Terrible torture commenced. Worst to suffer was Victor Tretyakevich who had been named in Pocheptsov's testimony as the ringleader of the organisation. The brave young girls and boys were strung up by their necks from window frames, their fingers were squeezed in doors, they were flogged with cudgels and whipped with cord, needles were driven under their finger and toe nails. The office of Solikovsky who conducted the interrogation looked more like a slaughter-house with all the blood covering the floor and walls. But nothing brought the Young Guards to their knees.

On the night of January 15, 1943, the first thirteen were hurled down the pit of No. 5 mine. They included Victor Tretyakevich, Ivan Zemnukhov, Ulyana Gromova and Anatoly Popov. January 16 was to have been Anatoly Popov's nineteenth birthday. On the 15th, when he had recovered consciousness after a round of torture, he wrote a letter in blood to his mother, which he succeeded in getting through via a policeman. For the next few days the police carted groups of underground fighters to the mine, shot them and bundled their bodies down the 250 foot pit-shaft of No. 5 mine. After Krasnodon's liberation, more than 70 unrecognisable corpses were retrieved from the mine.

Some of the Young Guards were shot in the park of the town of Rovenka. They included Oleg Koshevoi and Lyubov Shevtsova. The latter was arrested on January 8 in Lugansk where she had gone to contact the partisans. The nazis tortured her for more than a month trying to get information about the whereabouts of the wireless set and a code table which she was going to use to contact the partisan H.Q. On February 9, 1943, two days before the flight from the town of Rovenka, having forced nothing out of the young scout, the local S.S. chief, Drevitz, shot Lyuba through the head.

By decree of the Presidium of the Supreme Soviet of the U.S.S.R. of September 13, 1943, the leaders of the Young Guard—Ulyana Gromova, Ivan Zemnukhov, Oleg Koshevoi, Sergei Tyulenin and Lyubov Shevtsova were posthumously awarded the titles of Hero of the Soviet Union.

INSCRIPTION ON A Y.C.L. CARD
BELONGING TO SERGEANT GRIGORY KAGAMLYK

February 9, 1943

Dying, but not a step back. Vow with my own blood.
Serg. Kagamlyk

Grigory Kagamlyk, born in the Ukraine in 1923, was commander of an anti-tank gun section of the 3rd Company of the 47th Infantry Regiment, 15th Sivash Infantry Division.

It was the second year of the war on Soviet territory. The Soviet Army, having gained the initiative in the battle on the Volga, con-

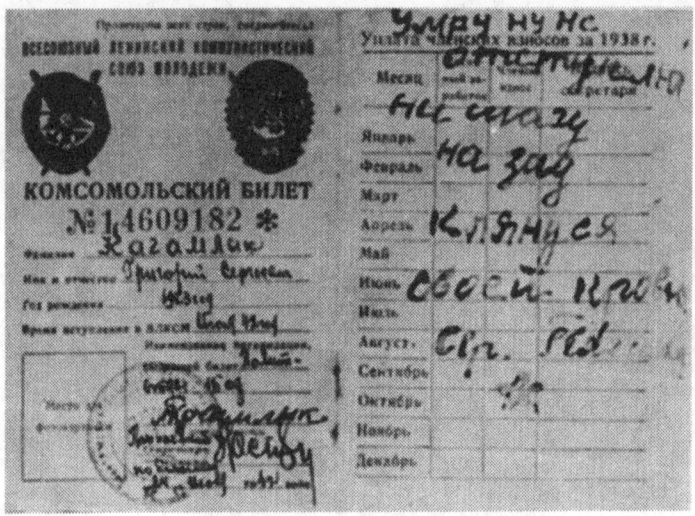

Y.C.L. card of Grigory Kagamlyk

tinued its westward drive. At the end of January and the beginning of February, 1943, Soviet troops on the Voronezh and Bryansk fronts routed a 125,000-strong contingent of enemy troops consisting of eleven German and two Hungarian infantry divisions and liberated Voronezh, Kursk and Belgorod.

On February 9, the Soviet advance cleared the Germans out of the village of Nikolsk in the neighbourhood of Kursk. The foe was determined to regain this crucial point, and Sergeant Kagamlyk and his anti-tank section were given the job of covering the right flank which spelled most danger. Enemy tanks with submachine-gunners trailing them bore down on the Soviet trenches. In the ferocious encounter that ensued Sergeant Kagamlyk was wounded three times. Despite an attempt to carry him back behind the lines, he stayed at his post and continued fighting. In a breather between attacks the sergeant, rapidly losing blood, jotted down a few words on his Y.C.L. card.

He was finally struck down by a bullet, but his resolve and fearlessness inspired his men, and they beat back the enemy. He was posthumously awarded the title of Hero of the Soviet Union and his name was put on his regiment's roll of honour.

Grigory Kagamlyk, Hero of the
Soviet Union

NOTE
OF FOUR DEFENDERS OF VOLCHANSK

Late February 1943*

We defenders of Volchansk died a brave death on this spot. There were four of us: Kozodub V., Bondarenko V., Sinin, Kiparenko T. Serg.

1943. Get the note to the airfield.

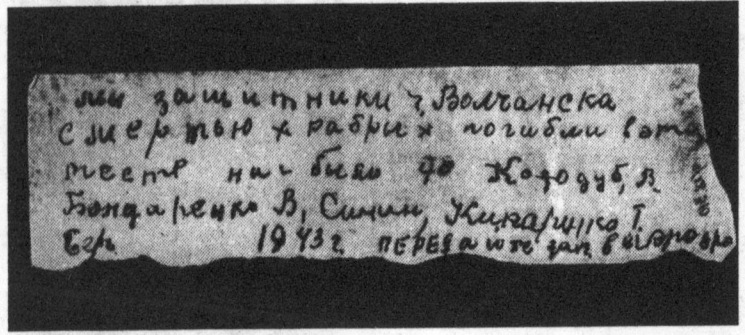

Note of the four defenders of Volchansk

In the summer of 1959, a local man from the town of Volchansk, near Kharkov in the Ukraine, N. Akulichev, spotted the tip of a metal canister peeping out of the sand on the site of what used to be an airfield. After digging it out, he noticed a number of openings on its

---

* Date of battle for Volchansk.

sides and in one of them a length of vinyl insulation with the word "Note" faintly scribbled on it. Inside lay a neatly folded slip of cigarette paper bearing in ink the last words and surnames of four men who fought and died defending Volchansk in 1943.

After the Soviet drive on Kharkov between February 2 and 16, 1943, the nazi High Command desperately tried to retake the initiative and avenge their recent defeats. They brought up over thirty divisions from the Western front and in late February undertook a counter-drive in the Donbas-Kharkov area. With these reinforcements the Germans pushed the Soviet troops back across the North Donets River. By the end of the month Soviet forces had to quit Kharkov, too, after a round of heavy fighting.

The enemy was not given a chance to surround the Soviet troops in the vicinity of Kharkov and take revenge for the defeat in the Battle of the Volga. It was probably about this time that the Volchansk defenders, beating off enemy tank attacks, wrote their note.

LETTER
FROM MEDICAL ORDERLY
VALENTINA KOLESNIKOVA

Not later than March 3, 1943*

Dear comrades at the front, my dearest friend Nina,

If I die in this battle, please let my mother know that I, her daughter, honourably carried out my duty to my country.

What a terrible pity my life has to end so early, but there are others to avenge me.

Nina, I was a nurse. That really is wonderful—to save the life of someone fighting for us, defending our homeland from the treacherous foe, struggling for our future.

That's about all, please let my mother know.

Valya Kolesnikova

Address: Lenin Collective Farm, Blagoveshchensky District, Altai Territory.

Like many other Soviet girls, Valentina Kolesnikova wanted to get to the front as quickly as possible. After finishing a nursing course, Valya was posted to the front. She received her combat baptism in the August skirmishes of 1942.

Scorning death which lurked everywhere she selflessly did her duty bringing aid to the wounded under the roar of guns, the whistling of shells and the blast of enemy mortars. She was always in the very thick of the danger.

On March 3, 1943, her young life was cut short by an enemy bullet during the fighting for Smolensk.

---

* Date of her death.

LETTER
FROM 15-YEAR-OLD KATYA SUSANINA

March 12, Liozno, 1943

Dear, kind Daddie,

I am writing to you from German captivity. When you read this letter, Daddie, I shan't be alive any more. I ask one thing of you, Father—punish the German rats. This is the last testament of your dying daughter.

A few words about mother. When you return, don't look for mummie. The Germans shot her. When they were asking questions about you, the officer lashed her across the face. Mummie couldn't take it any longer and proudly said, these are her last words: "You won't scare me with your beatings. I know my husband will come back and kick you dirty swine out of here." And the officer shot mummie right in the mouth. . . .

Dear Daddie, I am fifteen today, and if you met me now, you wouldn't recognise your little girl. I've got very skinny, my eyes are sunken, my curls have been sheared off, my hands have withered, I'm as skinny as a rake. Every time I cough, blood comes up—they've burst my lungs.

Do you remember the time, Daddie, two years ago, when I was thirteen? What a lovely birthday I had! I remember you saying to me then: "Grow up, my little girl, to all the joys in the world!" We played some records, our friends wished me Happy Birthday and we sang our favourite Young Pioneers' song.

125

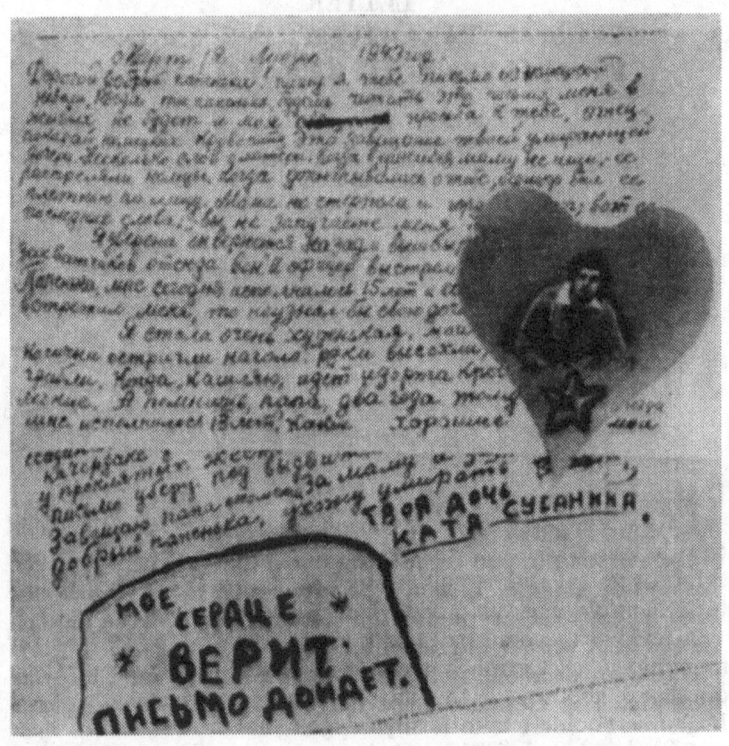

The first and the last pages of Katya Susanina's letter

But now, Daddie, when I look at myself in the mirror—my dress is torn, in rags, a number on my neck like a convict, I'm just a bag of bones—and salty tears are oozing from my eyes. What's the use of being fifteen. I'm no good to anyone. There are many people here no good to anyone. The starving wander about and are hunted down by sheepdogs. Every day they are taken out and murdered.

Yes Daddie, I am the slave of a German baron, I work for a German, Scharlen, as a laundrymaid, I wash the linen, scrub the floors. I work very hard and eat twice a day from a trough with Rosa and Klara—they are the mistress's swine. Those are the baron's orders. "Russians were and always will be pigs," he said. I'm very scared of Klara. She is a big and greedy pig. Once she nearly bit my finger off for grabbing a potato out of the trough.

I live in a shed—I'm not allowed in the room. Once Jósefa, the Polish chambermaid, gave me a crust of bread and the mistress caught her doing it and gave her a good lashing about her head and back.

Twice I ran away from them but the watchman discovered me both times. The baron himself ripped my dress off and kicked me until I fainted. Then they threw a pail of water over me and hurled me into the cellar.

Today I learned some news: Jósefa said my owners are leaving for Germany with a big group of men and women slaves from the Vitebsk District. They are taking me with them as well. No, I won't go with them to that infernal hell of a Germany. I've made up my mind that it's better to die on my native soil than be trampled into horrible German earth. Only death can rescue me from a cruel beating.

I don't want to suffer any more in the hands of these savage, ruthless Germans who won't let me live!

I beg you, Daddie, get revenge for mummie and me. Goodbye, kind daddie, I am leaving you, to die.

Your daughter

Katya Susanina

My heart tells me this letter will reach you.

Soon after the liberation of the Byelorussian town of Liozno in 1944, while clearing the brick work of a ruined oven in one of the houses, a small yellow envelope sown up with thread was found. The envelope contained a letter from a young Byelorussian girl, Katya Susanina, who had been taken in bondage to a German landowner. In the grip of despair Katya had committed suicide on her fifteenth birthday. Before dying she had written her last letter to her father. On the envelope was the following address: Active Army, Field Post No. . . . Pyotr Susanin. On the other side were the words in pencil: "Whoever finds this letter hidden from the Germans, I beg of you, please post it at once. My corpse will already be swinging from a rope."

The number of the field post had worn away with time and the letter was unable to find its mark, but it went to the hearts of all Soviet people. The letter was published in *Komsomolskaya Pravda* on May 27, 1944.

VICTOR CHALENKO'S TESTAMENT

Not later than March 14, 1943

If I die in combat for the workers' cause, I ask officers Vernishin and Kunitsyn to take the first opportunity they have to go to my home in Yeisk and tell my mother that her son died for the liberation of his country. Please let my dear mother have my order, my Y.C.L. card and this pad. Ask her to keep them as a memory of her son. Give her my sailor's hat so that she will have something to remember her sailor-boy by.

Mother's address: Raissa Chalenko, Svanovskaya St.,

Yeisk

Victor Chalenko

Y.C.L. member Victor Chalenko volunteered in 1942. When the Soviet troops had to leave Yeisk he begged to be taken on in a marine detachment. While he was in the marines he took part in the defence of the Northern Caucasus. For his heroism and bravery in the battles around Goryachi Klyuch and Tuapse, he was awarded the Red Banner Order. In February 1943, he landed with the rest of his marine group at Novorossiisk, on the Black Sea coast.

It was not an easy place for battle. The enemy had had time to reinforce their positions and were causing the marines a lot of trouble, particularly in one section of the beach where a machine-gun in a log emplacement kept up rapid fire. Victor volunteered to silence it. Under cover of darkness, he crawled towards the log emplacement and hurled his hand grenades into it. The firing stopped at once but splinters from the grenade also ripped into the hero. Taking advantage of the silenced machine-gun, the marines took the German positions by storm. They found their comrade dead. In his pocket was discovered a writing pad with his testament on it.

LETTERS HOME
FROM PARTISAN-SCOUT VALENTIN MALTSEV

LETTER TO HIS FATHER

March 14, 1943

14.3.43. I have to leave in a hurry. There was no time to say good-bye, don't be cross. I won't be coming home any more, though it isn't really settled yet, but I won't be in Leningrad again. So, good-bye. I'll be battling away as long as my eyes can see! And never mind the circumstances or the rumours! Well, once more I shake your strong hand, and hug and kiss you. Till better days and a happy reunion,

Yours,

V.

LETTER TO HIS MOTHER AND SISTER

March 16, 1943

Dearest Mum and Irinka,

I am writing from Khvoinaya where I arrived on March 16 at 9 p.m. I might disappear for about a year, but don't worry, that's all part of the job. And don't hang out the funeral notices, because I've reckoned on being back for Irina's wedding and mother's silver wedding anniversary. That's all for now, and for some time. All my love and kisses to tide you over my absence. Ma, I wrote you a letter with all sorts of stories which you must read, but don't take it too much to heart. Eternal glory to the dead, let the living live on. All my love to you. Bye-bye.

Your loving son,

Valya

Valentin Maltsev died when he was only eighteen. The story of his life and his heroic death pays homage to the wonderful qualities of this remarkable young man.

Valentin lived in Leningrad. When war broke out, his father joined the people's volunteer detachment and his mother and youngest sister Irina were evacuated. The young lad refused to be evacuated. He wanted to stay behind and fight the nazis, but the army refused to take him. With some of his pals he used to keep a look-out on the roofs at night and put out incendiaries, saw that the black-out was observed, went to military training and then worked at the Compulsory Universal Military Training Centre.

He bravely bore up to the hardships of the blockade of Leningrad, the cold and the hunger, the constant air raids and the night raids. Not once did he lose heart. In July 1943, he was offered a mission as wireless operator behind enemy lines. He trained hard in a special intelligence school. In March 1943, he was attached to a group led by M. Lyapushev and smuggled across the front to the vicinity of Pskov.

After successfully completing their mission the group was ordered back to base. In August 1943, not far from the front line, they ran into another group carrying a wounded man. To obtain food for the wounded man, they turned off into the village of Petrovo. In the darkness they had not noticed there were police in the village. To cover the escape of his comrades, Valentin held off the police with a pistol for as long as he could. Finally, with only one bullet left, he turned his pistol on himself rather than fall into enemy hands. To the end of his young life he remained true to his favourite motto: "Guards die. but don't surrender."

APPEAL
FROM MIKHAIL GUZOVSKY TO THE INHABITANTS
OF OSIPENKO

March 1943

Comrades,

The fascist bastards are crawling away.

Comrades, don't let them carry off valuable property, our bread.

Burn, exterminate, strangle and kill these crawling bastards.

Hide yourselves from evacuation because whoever's with them is our enemy.

Death to Hitler's rats!

(Read and pass on)

Mikhail Guzovsky was one of the most active members of the underground organisation in the town of Osipenko. He distributed leaflets which he had written by hand. A few days before the German forces left the town, he was captured by the nazis who found some leaflets on him. He was shot two days before the arrival of the Soviet Army.

LETTER HOME
FROM PARTISAN-SCOUT OLGA RZHEVSKAYA

February 22-April 6, 1943

Olga Rzhevskaya. Age 20.

Obolonovets, Mutishchensky Village Soviet, Yelninsky District.

Died 27/2-43. (For consorting with the partisans.)

Whoever finds this, please forward it to my parents.

My dearest Mother,

Greetings from your daughter Olga. Mama, today, March 6th, makes two months since I last saw freedom, but what does it matter? My dear Mama, you probably heard that we were sent to Spas-Demensk from Yelnya on January 11. The investigation wound up on January 14 and the trial finished on January 23. Up to February 27, I was detained in Spas-Demensk. On February 27, they transferred me to the Roslavl prison where I am today. I don't know about you, but I suppose it's no use me expecting to see you, my dearest Mother, again. All you can do, Mama, is to treasure that sad day when we had to part. That was January 10th, 1943 (a Sunday) when I had to desert my home village and you, my darling Mother.

Dear Mama, I have one request of you: don't worry about me, look after your health. You can't get me back but you mustn't lose your health. After all you're all alone with no one to rely on. Maybe Dusya will come back. Maybe she's had better luck than I. Mama, I'll probably be condemned to die in Roslavl, though I thought it would be in Spas-Demensk. . . .

Mama, I must ask you once again not to grieve over me—you won't help yourself by doing so. And that's probably my fate. Mama dear, I am now only with Nina, the other three who have been taken with us were removed on February 14, we don't know where they've been taken—home or some-where else.

Dearest Mama, just now I'd give anything to hear just one little word from you, from all our family, then I would die peacefully. I know my fate but I can't help feeling sorry for you, my darling Mother.

Mama, please give my regards to Auntie Lena and her children—Dusya, Valya, Kolya, to Auntie Natasha and Nadya, and Katya, and to all our friends and relations. Mama, my dearest, I'm coming to the end and beg you again not to worry, I'm not the only one, there are many of us. My dear, dear Mother, once more kind regards from your daughter Olya.

Mama, if only the situation could suddenly change, I would have been back with you. How happy we would have been. But no, Mama, miracles don't happen in real life. One thing I ask, don't worry, look after yourself and don't be sorry for anything. . . .

Mama, I made a calendar out for April and am crossing off the days of my life.

Olga Rzhevskaya was a 20-year-old partisan-scout. At dawn on January 6, 1943, she fell into the hands of the nazis, who came across her when she was ill at her mother's home in the tiny Smolensk village of Obolono-vets. Despite the fact that she was unconscious, the soldiers dragged her in for questioning. After torturing her for four days and getting nowhere, the nazis packed her off to the town of Yelnya, and then on to Spas-Demensk. The abominable prison routine dragged on, daily interrogation and torment. While waiting to be shot, Olga wrote on her neckerchief: "Died February 22." Then she altered it to "February 23". Then she had to revise that date every day until February 27.

On that day, she was trans-ferred to Roslavl prison and her

Olga Rzhevskaya

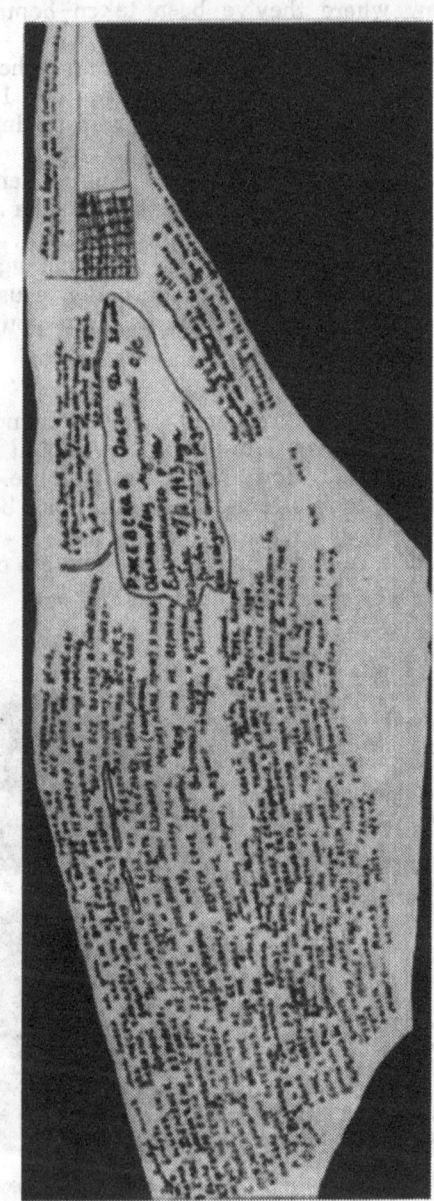

Olga Rzhevskaya's letter to her mother written on her neckerchief

daily count had to be started all over again. Every day the sick girl was dragged out for interrogation. One morning they took her out into the yard and stood her by the gallows.

"Now you can tell all!" said the officer. "In a minute you will be dead."

And she replied.

"I, Russian girl Olga Rzhevskaya, member of the Y.C.L. and a partisan, hate your guts. I've done everything I can to fight you. There are many like me. Your stores have been burnt down and are burning, your soldiers and officers are being killed, your communications cut—I've had a hand in it too. Pity I did so little. But I shall be avenged. Soon the Red Army will be here and...."

A kick from the officer's boot sent the stool under Olga's feet spinning, and Olga dangled from the rope. But that wasn't the end. The girl was pulled out of the noose, revived and shot a few days later.

The letter above was written in a prison cell between interrogation sessions. It was written in pencil in small writing on a white, silk neckerchief. In one corner is a calendar with the 30 days of April 1943. Only the first six days are crossed off.

LETTERS
FROM MEMBERS OF THE UNDERGROUND
Y.C.L. ORGANISATION IN DONETSK

SAVVA MATEKIN'S LETTERS TO HIS WIFE AND CHILDREN

August-October 5, 1942

Shura,

What can a man do when he's in the death cell? All the same they're scared of me. Tell that to our people. I know all's up with me and the moment will come quicker than we may expect. Good-bye. Please tell everybody this isn't the end. I die but you all live on.

Good-bye, my darling Shura

My dear little Vova and Lusya,

I've always strived to bring you up properly, make people out of you useful to the country, genuine, whole-hearted people. My greatest wish was to see you, Vovochka, a scholar, and you, Lusya, an engineer. But whatever you become I'm firmly convinced my children will not let their father down—he has not begrudged his life for the good of his country, for the sake of saving his people and for the happiness of his children. May you all be happy.

Your Father

I think my days are numbered. I hope you and the kiddies forgive me for everything. . . . Remember that I've always been ready to lay down my life for you. I die calm and confident. When you find it necessary, explain everything to the children —all the whys and the wherefores.

All my love to you for everything and from a pure heart. Forgive and forget and be happy.

3.10.42. Been through interrogation. Feel things will turn out for the worse, hurrying to relive all my short life again. Bring up the kiddies, look after yourself and keep smiling.

Yours,
Savva

STEPAN SKOBLOV'S LETTER

23-29 May, 1943

Farewell, dear friends,

I have to die at the age of 24. In the prime of life and creative thought the beating of my pulse has to come to a stop, and the hot blood has to cool in my veins. In the gaols of the German Gestapo I live out the last minutes of my life proudly, with head held high.

In these brief, oh too brief minutes I invest whole years, whole decades of unlived years, in these minutes I want to be the happiest man in the world, for my life has come to an end in the battle for human happiness. . . .

Farewell, dear comrades, farewell forever!

TESTAMENT OF 18 MEMBERS
OF THE UNDERGROUND ORGANISATION

May 29, 1943

Friends,

We die for a just cause. . . . Don't let it damp your spirit, stand up and flay the enemy at every turn. One request to all of you—don't forget our parents. . . .

Friends, listen to our call—flay the Germans! Farewell, you Russian people! Don't bear a grudge against us!

In the autumn of 1941, the nazi drive eastwards swept them over the Donets Basin. Together with other Soviet people who refused to surrender, the Y.C.L. members of the town of Donetsk took up arms against the foreign invaders. Their leader was Savva Matekin.

Savva Matekin was born in 1902. In the twenties, when life was just getting back to normal in the Soviet Far North, he went off to the remote Jamal Peninsula to help look after children there. Then

Savva Matekin

he worked for several years in the remote corners of Siberia before returning eventually to his native Donbas. In September 1941, he left for the front and was taken prisoner during the retreat. He escaped and since the front was already too far off, he resolved to return to his home in Budyonnovka—a workers' estate just outside Donetsk. There he managed to take charge of studies in the local school No. 68, where he had worked before the war. But he never gave up the struggle. He decided to set up an underground organisation from the teachers and pupils on the estate. Unafraid of the Gestapo, he and his two colleagues, Stepan Skoblov and Boris Orlov, formed a Y.C.L. resistance group.

In the autumn of 1941, a member of the group, Vasily Goncharenko got hold of their first six rifles and three boxes of ammunition. The group grew in number. Two months later the group numbered 42 young people. Inspired by their example, other underground groups in other estates began to function around Donetsk. After several raids on nazi soldiers they had a good supply of arms and ammunition. At the beginning of 1942, the resistance men and women blew up a railway bridge, put out of action the power station in Kurakhovka, damaged enemy vehicles, sabotaged food supplies, destroyed fuel dumps, attacked nazi soldiers and derailed several trains. Once, Vanya Klimenko and Volodya Kirilov were responsible for sabotaging a score of enemy vehicles waiting to be transported to the front from Mushketovo railway station.

The resistance fighters put out a special appeal to the Donetsk workers. They wrote: "At every mine, on every estate

Stepan Skoblov

and in every village, form partisan units, aid the partisans, hide them from the police, don't let the nazis carry off to Germany our grain, industrial and other equipment. Whether you work in the mines, at factories or in offices, hamper the German authorities from carrying out their orders and plans, do all you can to harm the Germans, spoil the equipment and output, get ready to welcome the Red Army with honour!"

In August 1942, Savva Matekin, the organiser and inspirator of the underground fighters, was arrested. Almost two months of torture could not break his will. On October 7, 1942, the Germans shot him at the Kalinovskaya mine.

On May 22, 1943, the Gestapo arrested 18 men. They were put through the usual grilling in the building of the field gendarmerie in Avdotino. Although they realised their fate was sealed, the young Soviet patriots courageously bore all their sufferings without a murmur. On the eve of their sentence they wrote a joint last testament to their friends.

Between May 30 and June 3, the entire 18 were shot. They included Stepan Skoblov and Boris Orlov. But the battle was not over. The underground organisation continued to take revenge on the Germans for the death of their comrades. Friends and comrades stepped into the shoes of the dead.

Savva Matekin's letter was written on scraps of paper in which his wife had wrapped a bottle of *kvass*. She had brought the bottle to the gaol and then had taken it back. The condemned man had thrown another part of his last notes into a ditch while on his way to work. His wife had followed at a short distance and picked them up. The last testament of the 18 was written in black pencil on a handkerchief.

До свиданія, дорогіе друзья. Я умираю на 24 году жизни. В результате сил и творческой мысли должны приостановиться біеніе моего пульса, а в жилах застынет горячая кровь. В застенках немецкого ГЕСТАПО последніе минуты своей жизни я доживала гордо и смело. В эти короткіе, слишком короткіе минуты я вкладывало целые годы, целые девятки недописанных лет, в эти минуты я хочу быть самым счастливым человеком в мире, ибо моя жизнь окончилась в борьбе за общечеловеческое счастье

A page from Stepan Skoblov's last letter to his friends from the prison

NOTE
FROM SERGEANT TIKHON BURLAK

Not later than June 1, 1943

I die for my country. Consider me a Communist. Please tell Lena I kept my promise and her love has gone with me.

Heavy fighting was in progress on the Eastern Front. The Germans were holding fast to their lines but the Soviet forces doggedly pushed ahead. During the liberation of the village of Medveditsa, one soldier wiped out eight nazis. Weak, wounded, and losing a lot of blood, Sergeant Burlak seized an enemy submachine-gun and a stock of hand grenades and again rushed into the fighting.

After the battle, Tikhon Burlak was taken to hospital, but was soon back in the trenches with his unit. He used to tell his comrades, both old and new, about his girl-friend and once mentioned that none of his family had remained alive in his Ukrainian home town of Nikolayev.

One fine spring day, Sergeant Burlak was machine-gunning the Germans from a gun emplacement.

Several times that day the Germans threw everything they had into the attack, but each time the brave sergeant and his machine-gun blocked their way. Towards nightfall, the fighting abated. But early on the following day the Germans tried to overrun the sergeant's post once again. Certain there was a large group of Soviet machine-gunners in the bunker, the Germans called up a bomber to snuff out the fire. Bombs and shells gradually reduced the bunker to a churned-up morass. Somehow the sergeant survived, although towards evening he was wounded in the arm and head. But he stayed at his post. He continued to fight as long as his ammunition held out. At long last, after three days of fighting he was left with only two hand grenades and a flare. Tikhon Burlak fired a flare which lit up the Germans and hurled one grenade into the very thick of the Germans. The other he dropped under himself, blowing him and his machine-gun to smithereens.

By dawn the nazis were repelled and the battle was won. Around the bunker lay 48 nazi corpses.

The Soviet soldiers rushed into what was once the bunker and found their comrade's remains.

Near the tangled mass of the machine-gun lay the familiar photograph of Lena, spattered with spots of fresh blood and punctured by a grenade splinter.

On the ground also lay a note written in large blood-stained letters on a sheet of paper by the dead hero—Sergeant Tikhon Burlak.

LETTER
FROM PARTISAN COMMANDER
VASILY SHIMANSKY TO HIS WIFE

Not later than June 1, 1943

To my life's companion and work colleague, my darling, my eternally unforgettable, dear Esfir Kharitonovna.

From Starik (V. A. Shimansky), commander of a partisan detachment.

Dear Esfir Kharitonovna,

It will soon be two years since the barbarians first attacked our sacred land and broke up the peaceful, happy life of many millions of Soviet people. Broke up, too, our family life. I am certain it will take less time than has already passed for the Soviet people, and us included, to restore our former happy life. What's more, everyone, including you and I, will rebuild our lives on an even higher level than before. For over the last couple of years, everyone has learned a lot about the necessity of valuing time in life and life in time, about the necessity of valuing your life's companion and yourself as a companion.

Darling Firochka, I learned a terrific amount when I was training and under the wing of our country, but I learned a lot more when I took up my rifle and went to defend the country. I'm a different man now. Not at all the one you knew before. Now I've spilled a lot of fascist blood and aged awfully.

143

I'm helping the country from without, and I so much want to help you, too, even if it isn't very much. Don't know how, my darling, everything's been given up to the country. Perhaps the time will soon come when we shall meet and tell each other everything, help each other and begin to live as people do in paradise. That day will be happy for us all because it will be simply wonderful, like nothing on earth.

Darling Firochka, I've been working behind the lines and I'm glad to say I've been able to obtain extremely valuable documents on the exact location of the major nazi airfield on the South-Eastern Front, the chief base of the Luftwaffe H.Q. on the South-Eastern Front and the chief headquarters of Göring who is often visited there by Hitler. With these documents in my hands, I handed over my partisan command and will soon be crossing the front myself. It's a very dangerous mission, but, with a bit of luck, it can be accomplished.

I put myself at my country's disposal, knowing that if I can get these documents through to the Soviet Government, it will go some way to driving the nazis out of the Ukraine and be a particularly severe blow at their Air Force. Besides, I have to get orders as to the further activities of my detachment. Things are going from bad to worse with the detachment. I have to know our future plan of action.

Good-bye, darling Firochka, I've left Marusya documents on the detachment's activities. If I die please see that these documents get through to the Soviet Government and consider me a partisan of the war.

Good-bye, my dearest darling, my true love Esfir Kharitonovna. Let all my friends and acquaintances know I have given everything for the country's defence.

On June 1, 1943, I shall part with Nastya and in a month's time should be with you, if not—the grave will have swallowed me up.

Good-bye, darling,

Good-bye, all my friends,

Good-bye, to you, too, my dear Motherland,

Starik

Vasily Shimansky was born in 1902 in the town of Balta not far from Odessa. Once a farm labourer, he graduated in the thirties from the Plekhanov Economic Institute in Moscow. In 1938, he took up a post-graduate course. After a successful defence of his thesis, he was appointed lecturer of political economy in the Plekhanov Institute.

In August 1941, Vasily Shimansky left for the front.

In December of the same year he turned up under the name of Pyotr Lishchenko in Kordelevka, not far from Vinnitsa. After getting a job as blacksmith at a sugar refinery, he became friends with ex-prisoners-of-war who had escaped from camps and were living in Kordelevka. Three of the ex-p.o.w.s—Andrei Yevtukhov, Eduard Lyakhovetsky and Victor Trishin—joined the Old Man (Starik), as Shimansky was known because of his beard, in forming an underground group.

Starik's group went into action. In order to study the approaches to the main rail lines, Shimansky became a shepherd.

Vasily Shimansky

Soon after, the underground fighters derailed a fuel-carrying train. Their numbers grew. Besides the group in Kordelevka other groups sprang up, including one at the local state farm of Katerinovka, all uniting in Starik's partisan detachment.

In a single year they several times tore up the track on the Vinnitsa-Kiev line, derailed enemy trains, blew up vehicles, fuel dumps, burned grain and killed cattle about to be dispatched to Germany, set fire to nazi-occupied buildings, etc.

The detachment discovered the location of Göring's headquarters and a large German air base situated nearby. They also came upon Hitler's lair known under the code name of Wehrwolf.

At the beginning of May 1943, the underground fighters took to the Chorni (Black) Forest where they joined up with another partisan unit. Meanwhile Vasily Shimansky and three companions moved on to the east, towards the front. In mid-May, after several days and nights of hard and torturous travel, the four men, wracked by wounds and fatigue, came to the village of Kozatskoye, a few miles from Balta. Here they were hidden by the local villagers, relations of Shimansky. After a rest and medical treatment, they struggled on to cover the last few miles at the end of May. What happened after that is unknown.

Vasily Shimansky left behind with Maria Oleinik a number of documents addressed to Soviet Army Command, and his last letter to his wife, published above. The documents had been put in a bottle and buried in the ground. After liberation, Maria Oleinik handed over the documents to the Soviet authorities.

NOTE
FROM FIVE DEFENDERS OF GLAZUNOVKA

Whoever finds this note, please report our deaths. There are five of us left, our ammunition has run out, all we have are three dozen grenades. Enemy tanks have appeared in the distance. Farewell, dear comrades, we have died for our Soviet motherland.... 12.VI.1943. V. Boiko, A. Kravchenko, G. Vetrov, V. Yablochkin, A. Siyanovsky.

On August 30, 1961, a young schoolboy, Zhenya Kistanov, while playing near his home near the Glazunovka drying works, found a cartridge case, mildewed with age. Inside the case he discovered a tightly rolled piece of paper from a note-book on which the gallant five's last words had been inscribed. They had apparently taken part in the battle on the Kursk-Orlov Bulge.

After the publication of the note in the central newspapers the pupils of Glazunovka secondary school received many letters from those who had taken part in this great battle and from relations of the dead five. Ex-soldiers wrote of the bloody encounters that had taken place in the summer of 1943 in the neighbourhood of Glazunovka. Units of the Central front had beaten off attacks of enemy tanks and self-propelled guns.

NOTE
FROM Y.C.L. GIRL MARIA KISLYAK
FROM KHARKOV GESTAPO GAOL

Not later than June 18, 1943

Comrades,

I die for my country, without grudging my life. Good-bye, dear sister Natasha and Mum and Dad.

Maria

On June 18, 1943, in the village of Lyodnoye, just outside Kharkov, the nazis hanged three young patriots: Maria Kislyak, 18 years old, Fyodor Rudenko, 19, and Vasily Bugrimenko, 19.

The daring youngsters had not bowed to the "New Order" and had thrown all they had into resistance to the S.S. The eldest of the trio, Fyodor Rudenko was not yet twenty years of age and Maria Kislyak had only just graduated from Kharkov medical school.

During the first occupation of Kharkov, Maria Kislyak concealed and nursed in her flat two wounded soldiers who later rejoined the Soviet forces after Kharkov's liberation in February 1943.

In the spring of 1943, Lyodnoye was captured for the second time. The two boys and a girl formed an underground group. Fyodor Rudenko already knew a few things about war as he had volunteered for the army in February 1943, had been

Maria Kislyak

Maria Kislyak's note from the Kharkov Gestapo gaol

taken prisoner near Chuguyev, escaped and came home to Lyodnoye where he had at once joined the underground group.

In late May 1943, the three were arrested and packed off to the Gestapo in Kharkov. For over a fortnight the Gestapo tortured the youngsters and on June 18 brought them, battered but undefeated, to Lyodnoye for a public hanging. Before the hanging, Fyodor Rudenko was unable to say a word since the nazis had gagged him. But Maria Kislyak shouted: "Good-bye, Mum and Dad and all my friends, I die for my country. Comrades, kill the Germans, purge our soil of these evil creatures."

A note from Maria scribbled on a piece of paper was smuggled from the Kharkov Gestapo gaol.

FROM A LETTER
WRITTEN BY INTELLIGENCE MAN
NIKOLAI KUZNETSOV

July 24, 1943

Tomorrow marks eleven months behind enemy lines.

On August 25, 1942, at 24.05, I was dropped by parachute to spare the Germans no mercy in revenge for the blood and tears shed by our mothers and brothers who groan under the yoke of German occupation.

Eleven months I've been scrutinising the enemy with the aid of a German officer's uniform. I've been preparing a fatal blow, having got into the very lair of the satrap—Erich Koch, the German tyrant in the Ukraine.

My mission is vital and to carry it through I have to sacrifice my life, since getting away from the city centre after making my attempt at the enemy during the parade is completely out of the question. I love life, I'm still very young. But because my motherland, whom I love like my own mother, requires that I lay down my life in the name of freedom from German occupation, I shall do so. Let the whole world know the spirit and fire of a Russian patriot and Bolshevik. Let the nazi gangleaders remember that trying to conquer our people is like trying to put out the sun.

German bastards like Hitler, Koch and company thought they could destroy our great Soviet nation. They had some dim-witted idea about drowning the Russian and other fraternal peoples of the U.S.S.R. in a sea of blood.

They forgot or didn't know history, these savages of the 20th century. They will understand all right on July 29, 1943, when after a whistle an anti-tank grenade will explode spilling their pagan German blood all over the asphalt. . . . Even if I die, my people will keep my memory eternal.

"You may die, but in the song of the brave and the strong in heart, you will forever be a living example, a proud appeal for liberty and reason."

That comes from my favourite piece of Gorky, I wish our young people would read it more often. That's where I got my strength for great deeds.

Yours,

Kuznetsov

To be read only after my death.

24/VII. 1943 Kuznetsov

Nikolai Kuznetsov was born in 1911 in the village of Zyryanka near Chelyabinsk in the Urals. Not far from his native village was a German colony. The young Nikolai often used to come and chat with the German colonists in German. Before he finished school he spoke German quite fluently.

Up to 1938, he lived in Komi-Perm territory, and later went to work at the Uralmash plant in Sverdlovsk.

When war came he was working in Moscow as an engineer at a motor works. In the first few days of war he made a request to be sent behind the lines on intelligence work. In May 1942, he began to get ready for action in the enemy's rear under the guise of a German officer. He first went through a tough training course, learning about German arms and army procedure, sharpening up his shooting and studying explosives, and talking with captured German officers.

On the night of August 25, 1942, Nikolai Kuznetsov and a tiny band of paratroopers landed behind enemy lines. Three days later, Kuznetsov met up with D. Medvedev, commander of a partisan detachment and a Hero of the Soviet Union. That marked the commencement of the activities of the famous scout.

Kuznetsov several times successfully carried out daring missions and from October 1942 he spent most of his time in the town of Rovno, the residence of Erich Koch, Reichskommissar for the Ukraine.

In the very heart of the nazi administration of the Ukraine, Kuznetsov carried out exception-

Nikolai Kuznetsov, Hero of the
Soviet Union

ally brave and daring missions. He was often instrumental in getting through to the Soviet Command extremely valuable political and military information. With his help, for example, the Soviet authorities managed to uncover a plot by the nazi intelligence to assassinate the heads of government of the anti-Hitler coalition during the Teheran Conference in 1943.

Nikolai Kuznetsov was an exceedingly courageous and clever man. His exploits were truly legendary. Once, dressed as a nazi officer, he got into the building of a German court and shot dead the chief nazi judge in the Ukraine Alfred Funk. At the end of September 1943, he carried out a death sentence order passed by the partisans on Paul Dargel, Koch's assistant for political affairs, and General Hermann Knut, another of Koch's right-hand men.

In November 1943, he and three comrades smuggled out of his private residence General Ilgen, commander of Germany's special forces in the Ukraine.

On January 18, 1944, Nikolai Kuznetsov received new instructions and left for Lvov to assassinate the butcher of the Ukrainian people—Deputy Governor of Galicia, Bauer. Mission completed, Kuznetsov and two partisans—Jan Kaminsky and Ivan Belov—made their way to the front. During the night of March 8, 1944, in the village of Boratin near Lvov, they were recognised by one of the Bendera gang. In the ensuing skirmish Nikolai Kuznetsov blew up himself and the onrushing foe with a hand grenade.

On November 5, 1944, he was posthumously awarded the title of Hero of the Soviet Union.

The published letter was written on July 24, 1943, in the event of his death.

INSCRIPTION
BY MARINA GRYZUN ON THE WALL
OF HER CELL

July 28, 1943

I, Y.C.L. girl Marina Gryzun, was shot by the Germans on July 28, 1943. Friends and comrades, avenge me and all those who have died in German hands!

Marina Gryzun had lived all her life on the Lenin Collective Farm in the village of Misailovka near Kiev. During the nazi occupation she hid and nursed three Red Army men who had remained behind the lines. Together with other Y.C.L. members she wrote leaflets calling on everyone to fight the invaders, and stuck them on house walls. She carried on agitation among the local inhabitants. In June 1943, Marina was arrested and shut up in a Gestapo cell in Boguslav. The Germans cruelly tortured her. The reprisal against her was carried into effect on July 28. The words above were inscribed in blood on the cell wall.

LETTER HOME AND NOTE
FROM ALEXANDRA POSTOLSKAYA

LETTER HOME

November 1942

I'm getting on all right. Life in the army is grand. You feel you are a real human being and you change an awful lot.

After the war I'll carry on my peacetime job, but for the moment I'm a real soldier girl. You wouldn't recognise me now. Soon I'll send you a photo of me!

Well, that's all for now.

I wish I could get just a couple of lines from you. Please write, dear Tanya, you know yourself what it's like to get no news for nearly six months.

Mummy, don't you go worrying about all of us. You should be proud that the son and daughter you brought up are serving in the Red Army. You certainly know how much our country needs us!

Keep calm, darling Mummy, when the time comes your children will never let you down, just as you taught us, just as the Y.C.L. taught us.

And if we have to die, then we shall die like the hundreds and thousands of our glorious men at the front.

After all, how many young girls and boys give their lives to save their country, how many wonderful, decent people fearlessly fight and bravely fall in battle, but never surrender!

Isn't that an inspiration to us all!

And our duty, duty to all our people, is to learn to be good soldiers and become fully-fledged fighters for the Red Army.

Don't be sad, Mummy! Not one of the beasts will remain on our soil!!!

All for now.

Please write, Tanyusha. Look after mum and little Vera. Lots of love to you all,

Yours loving,
Shura

NOTE

If I die, please let my father know that I fulfilled his order as befits a Communist.

Alexandra

9.8.1943

When she entered her first year in the Tomsk Polytechnical College, Alexandra Postolskaya was full of happy dreams of the future. But war came and sharply revised all her plans.

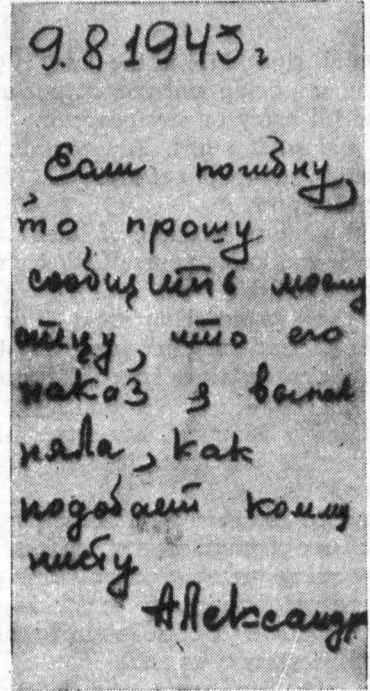

The last words of A. Postol-skaya's letter

Following in the footsteps of her father, Sergei Postolsky, and her brother Vladimir, the teenager volunteered for the army in the spring of 1942.

News about her acceptance into the army came as a great thrill: "They trust me, I'm going to the front," she wrote at the time. "I love my country, love life.... And I'll help the army and the front. How marvellous!!!"

It was not long before Shura was in the thick of the fighting with the 758th Rifle Regiment.

In July 1943, things began to hot up at the front as the nazis brought up fresh reinforcements. Her battalion had to fight desperately and without any let-up in order to shield some of the neighbouring units.

Alexandra Postolskaya

In the vicinity of the village of Rybka, near Smolensk, the battalion made a counter-attack, several times engaging large enemy forces. On the night of August 9, 1943, the battalion soldiers found themselves ringed off. It was then that Shura wrote her last note in which she affirms she has done her duty as befits a Communist.

After receiving instructions to pierce the enemy ring, Shura and a group of scouts searched for weak links in the enemy encirclement, and when a suitable place was found, she was the first to rush at the Germans with the battle cry: "Kill the beasts!" Behind her came the scouts and a platoon of submachine-gunners. The Germans wavered, then gave way. The soldiers tore through the breach and quickly rejoined their unit.

On August 16, 1943, the German Command started a new offensive. New waves of enemy soldiers threw themselves against the battalion's position. Again it was faced with the danger of being cut off. Alexandra Postolskaya, seeing that the enemy had almost broken through on the left flank, rushed across to lend a hand. Her submachine-gun fire flailed the frantic Germans. For a brief second she laid down her gun, picked up hand grenades, and hurled them into their midst. "Forward, comrades!" shouted the young girl as she led her companions into a fresh counter-attack.

The Rybka fighting lasted several hours and ended in victory. But the soldiers' rejoicing was marred by Alexandra's death.

LETTER
FROM JUNIOR LIEUTENANT LEONID KURIN
TO HIS SISTER

Not later than August 15, 1943

Hello there, Sonya. I'm sending you my battle greetings and wish you and your children a happy and carefree life.

Sonya, my dear sister, there's so much I would like to tell you about in these lines, so many thoughts I'd like to share with you.

The war's already been on for many months. Throughout these terrible days of fighting for our country, I have borne my name of Communist and Soviet patriot with honour. I've experienced the dangers and hardships of war but I've also tasted the sweet smell of victory. It's just a pity that I haven't killed enough Germans. But I've chalked up a few successes: four enemy planes shot down and 150 or so enemy soldiers have bit the dust from my bullets. If I live longer I'll try to notch up a few more, really give the enemy something to think about. But if I die, my comrades-in-arms will make them pay for my death, they'll give Fritz something to remember us by for the torments to my country, for the suffering of the Russian people, and for me.

Sonya, I've been thinking about death—is it so awful or not? No, it isn't so awful when you die for the future happy days, for the happiness of our children. But a life has to be given at the price of ten from the enemy. I am following in father's footsteps. He was killed in 1919 and I have kept his tradition. He fought for my life. I am fighting for the lives of your children.

Sonya, I'd give anything to be home, if only for one short day, just to see you. I know things are not so easy with you, but you have to get over them somehow, take them all in your stride come what may. And you will be over the hump.

Give all the family my love, say hello to Kostya and Sasha for me. I hope they get on all right together. Kiss grannie and mother.

Please don't cry, I ask you one thing—remember I fought and died honourably, as befits a Russian and a Bolshevik. And to you, my childhood companion, Sophie my dear, I wish a long life and much happiness.

Farewell to you all. We shall win! Death to the German invaders!

Leonid

Wireless-operator and air-gunner Junior Lieutenant Leonid Kurin was fatally wounded in an air battle over Leningrad. A letter was found in his field-case addressed to his sister in Teikovo not far from Ivanovo. The note attached read: "Please post it in the event of my death." His fellow flyers sent a copy of the letter to the Leningrad newspaper *Smena* which published it on August 15, 1943.

NOTE
FROM THE GUARDS LIEUTENANT
MIKHAIL PANCHENKO

Not later than August 18, 1943

Dear comrades,

In a few minutes the Germans will come at us again. But they won't get through! If I happen to fall in this battle, please inform my girl-friend at the following address:

Valya Fufayeva, Povorino, Voronezh Region.

On a section of the Bryansk Front, an unequal battle was in progress with nazi infantrymen. Thirty enemy bombers pounded the trenches, heavy Tiger tanks approached and behind them came grey-green lines of German soldiers. A platoon of guards under Lieutenant Panchenko which had just had time to dig itself in took the full force of the onslaught. The Soviet soldiers met the onrushing infantry with a tornado of automatic and machine-gun fire. All the same, six tanks managed to get to the trenches. Lieutenant Panchenko halted one Tiger tank with an anti-tank grenade, the rest were destroyed by the artillery. Again the enemy attacked. The company commander was killed. Lieutenant Panchenko took over. Under the command of the courageous lieutenant the soldiers fought off 14 onslaughts and wiped out more than 200 men. In the last attack, Mikhail Panchenko was killed. His note, written during the fighting, was discovered in his tunic pocket.

LETTER
FROM MEDICAL ORDERLY
VALERIA GNAROVSKAYA

August 22, 1943

My dear little Vitya, Mummie and Grannie,

Haven't dropped you a line for a whole week—haven't had the time. Yesterday we came out of the fighting and there was a letter from Vitya waiting for me. So I am replying at once.

First a couple of words about myself—I'm alive and well. To tell you the truth, I don't hear very well at the moment, but it will blow over. I've already been twice in fighting. From 15.8.43 to 21.8.43 we've been giving the Gerries hell in these parts. They tried to knock us off of the hill we were holding but all their attempts to break through were foiled. Our lads fought hammer and tongs—all my dear and brave comrades true to their orders: not a step back.

Many of them died a hero's death, but I came through alive and, my dear ones, even if I say it myself, I think I didn't let anyone down. I carried about thirty badly wounded from the battlefield. The regimental commander mentioned me in the dispatches and I think he has put me forward for an award.

Dear Vitya, you write that things are pretty bad at home. I know, my love, but you must set your teeth, overcome all the difficulties and realise that all this is the doing of the dirty fascist beast. We have to show him what we are made of and get revenge on him for smashing our happy life, for hundreds and thousands of dead and wounded, and for the blood and tears of our fathers, mothers and sisters. You have never had occasion to feel uncomfortable for my sake. And I assure you that will never be necessary.

Look after yourselves, write more often.

Lots of kisses to all of you,

Valya

Valeria Gnarovskaya, Hero of the
Soviet Union

Valeria Gnarovskaya, a sweet and kind 19-year-old girl, was known
at the front as Little Swallow. Valya saved the lives of many wounded
soldiers.

Once, in September 1943, the nazis suddenly launched a desperate
assault on a section held by her regiment. Two Tiger tanks broke
through the defences and were bearing down on the regiment's position. It was a very critical moment. And then something happened
which even eyewitnesses find difficult to put into words. With a bundle
of grenades Valya ran forward and threw herself right under the
tracks of the leading Tiger. There was a big explosion and the tank
ground to a halt. The second tank tried to turn back but it was too
late. Valya's comrades dashed up and put it out of action. Thanks to
her self-sacrifice, the breach was quickly patched up, the assault beaten
off and the regiment put on the offensive. Valeria Gnarovskaya was
posthumously awarded the title of Hero of the Soviet Union.

LETTER
FROM SOVIET P.O.W.S
IN THE CHISTYAKOV WAR CAMP

Dear brothers, we believe you will soon arrive and probably find our letter. You will know that there was a concentration camp here. Not far from the camp, there stands a cross marking the remains of 7,000 Soviet people, shot or bayoneted or starved to death.... Something like 600 wounded prisoners have been murdered. We write to you just before our death. In five or ten minutes we shall also be killed....

Tell everyone about our fate. Get your revenge. Sensing the end is near, the fascists have gone mad torturing our people....

Farewell! They're coming for us.

With communist greetings,

Senior Lieutenant in the Medical Corps

K. Kh. Khamedov
Medical Instructor
Kurchenko
Red Army Man
Andreyev

August 30, 1943

When the Donbas was liberated in September 1943, Soviet soldiers discovered many cases of the awful trail of bestiality left by the Germans. Many mines in the Donets Basin had been turned into mass graves. This letter was written by three p.o.w.s in the Chistyakov concentration camp shot by the nazis before the retreat.

INSCRIPTION AND LETTER HOME
FROM INTELLIGENCE GIRL ZOYA KRUGLOVA

Not later than September 9, 1943

INSCRIPTION IN A CELL

I used to love freedom and the wide open spaces, that's why it's very hard to get used to being locked up. In Greek, my name, Zoya, means life. Oh, how I want to live, live, live. . . . Zoya Baiger (Kruglova).

LETTER HOME

My dear Mum and Dad, dear little sisters Valya, Panya and Shura and dear little brother Borya. I'm writing to you, darlings, from prison for the last time. You will receive this letter when I am dead.

My darlings, it's already a year since you received news from me; I've been wandering about all the time but I never forgot about you. They arrested me in February and that makes two and a half months since I've been here alone in a solitary cell. Every day I expected to be taken out and shot. Mummie, things have been pretty grim but I endured it all. They sent me to a camp in Pskov where I stayed two months and escaped back to our side. I was again sent on a mission and again I ended up in this prison—this is the second month. I have been beaten about the head with sticks. Now waiting to be shot. I don't think any more about living though, my dear ones, I very much want to live a bit if only to see you, give you a big hug and cry all my grief away on your breast, Mummie dear. In fact, if I hadn't landed here a second time I would have been home in September. But, there it is, it's no use crying over spilt milk. At least, I've done my duty.

My dear ones, you can be proud that I haven't besmirched your good name and honour. I am going to die, but I know what for.

Mummie, don't take it too badly, don't cry. I would have liked to have consoled you but I'm very far away and behind iron bars and thick walls. I frequently sing songs in gaol, and the whole prison listens. This is a song about my life and my sad end:

> Don't you weep, don't weep,
> > my darling,
> Don't you grieve my Mother dear.
> We shall beat the nazi bandits
> And be home again, don't fear.
> But she died without returning
> From her Ostrov prison cell.
> By night they came and took her,
> Shot her by the prison rail. ...

My dear ones, other girls will tell you about me, if they survive. ... Once more I beg you, please don't cry, don't despair. My last farewell to Auntie Liza, Uncle Vanya, Lena Almazova and every one of my friends, comrades and relatives.

All my love to you all.

Farewell forever.

My body will be in Ostrov behind the gaol by the side of the road. I shall be clothed in my black woollen dress, which is a bit faded now, and the red knitted jumper you bought for me, my dear Mummie, and Russian boots.

Your daughter,
Zoya
Good-bye, good-bye. ...

Zoya Kruglova was born on April 23, 1923, in the village of Moshen-skoye near Novgorod. She threw everything into the battle as soon as war broke out. Zoya took part in putting up defences and evacuat-ing children from Leningrad, taught the local population what to do during air raids and, at the same time, took a course in nursing. In the autumn of 1941, she was appointed medical orderly to the 145th Anti-tank Battalion. Shortly after, she began work for the intelligence on the North-Western Front.

In the winter of the same year, she joined up with Anna Dmitriyeva and wireless-operator Panya Morozova in crossing the front. The Soviet High Command sent the girls to Soshikhin District, not far

Zoya Kruglova

from Pskov, to gather information about nazi troop movements on the Leningrad front. Having a good command of German, Zoya passed herself off as a German girl, Baiger, whose father was supposed to have been shot by the Bolsheviks in 1938. She succeeded in finding out valuable information about landing strips, the number of garrisons and the movements of enemy troops. This information was radioed back to H.Q.

After spending a brief leave at home, Zoya once more went behind the lines. In the company of a new wireless-operator, Zinaida Baikova ("The Wonder-girl"), Zoya was flown to the town of Ostrov in the Pskov Region. Once in the town the girls managed to get hold of passports and find work: Zoya in a labour office and her friend as a cleaner in a military unit. The two girls made contact with the town underground and went into action. In November they transmitted four messages back to H.Q. After the arrest of underground leader Klava Nazarova, the nazis began to keep a closer watch on all suspects.

At the commencement to 1943, Kruglova and Baikova were seized by the Gestapo. Without getting anything out of the two girls, the Gestapo sent Kruglova to a camp for condemned prisoners in Pskov and Baikova off to the Düsseldorf prison in Germany.

Zoya escaped from the death prison and made her way back to the partisans, but as she was attempting to cross the front she fell into the hands of some provocateurs who passed as partisans and again found herself in the Ostrov gaol.

In the nazi cell, Zoya conducted herself bravely. For more than a month the nazis put the girl through various tortures. As a fellow prisoner, A. Poyarkova, later testified, the girl was often brought back from questionings with her head and face covered in blood and bruises, but her spirit never sagged. She would often lament: "Oh, how I want to live!" She never gave death a thought. Many a time when she would sing, silence would descend on the gaol while everyone listened to her songs.

Realising that this time there was no escape, Zoya did all she could to see that her parents received her last letter. With the aid of Dusya Demidova, she succeeded in sending a note to her sister whom she knew before her arrest. With the knowledge that her note had got through, Zoya sent her letter home in the same way.

At dawn on September 9, 1943, Zoya Kruglova was taken out with four members of the Ostrov underground and shot, four miles from the town, at a spot just off the main Ostrov-Palkino highway.

LETTERS
FROM MEMBERS
OF THE ZAPOROZHYE UNDERGROUND

BORIS ZHIVENKO'S LETTER TO HIS MOTHER

September 2, 1943

Dear Mum,

I've received all you sent but it looks like being all to no avail as we are to be shot before Sunday. Oh, my dear Mum, I so want to live. Let's have some apples today....

Kisses to all.

September 2, 1943

Boris

LEONID VINER'S LETTER TO HIS WIFE

September 5, 1943

Dear Shura,

It's all over, either today or tomorrow I'll be shot like the hundreds of others shot since September 1. Please believe me I go to my death for your sake because I love you and the children more than anyone ever loved. I've had a good deal of chances to taste freedom but I didn't take them out of love for you and the children. When the children grow up, please explain that to them. Kiss them for me, my darling, darling Shura.

Love and kisses to you. Bye-bye forever,

Leonid

September 14, 1943

We die like heroes.

Address: 26 Baranov St., Block 4, Voznesenka.

Whoever finds this, get it to my children.

All those in Gonchar's group were shot on 14.IX.43.

Viner

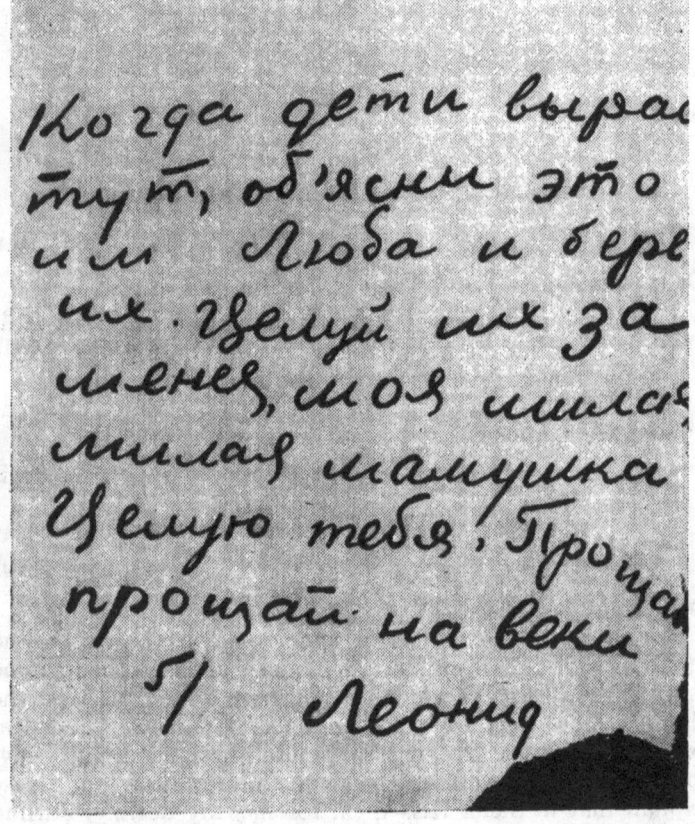

The last page of L. Viner's letter from prison to his wife

Leonid Viner

In April 1942, in the town of Zaporozhye in Orjonikidze District, an underground group was formed mostly made up of workers from Zaporozhstal, the local steel plant. Its ringleaders included Leonid Viner, A. Girya, Boris Zhivenko, Y. Ovsyuk (Kryukova), N. Stribkov (N. Khristenko) and A. Fokin. Leader of the group was Nikolai Gonchar. By June 1943 there were several dozen fighters in the group busy organising acts of sabotage, gathering arms and ammunition, distributing leaflets with news, arranging prison escapes and providing the escapees with clothing, food and false documents. Wireless sets hidden in the flats of Girya and Zhivenko supplied the group with Soviet news bulletins. In the summer of 1942, the conspirators built a secret tunnel in a well in Gonchar's yard. There they concealed their arms, literature and typed out leaflets.

The group did all they could to prevent their plant from being destroyed. To this end they got Gonchar appointed to the post of superintendent of the factory police. With his influence, Girya and other underground men were accepted into the factory police.

On June 28, 1943, forty of the group were given away due to poor conspiration technique and taken in custody. This terrible blow took off Gonchar, Viner, Girya and Zhivenko among others. When their flats were searched the wireless sets and secret passage came to light.

On September 14, 1943, the group's leader, Nikolai Gonchar, chief of operations Leonid Viner, Girya, Zhivenko and a number of other active members were shot after several sessions of excruciating torture. Before their death, the fearless patriots wrote letters home from the Gestapo prison. The two letters above safely reached their destination. Viner's note to the Soviet people was later found on him by other underground fighters after the shooting.

LETTER
FROM FLYER GRIGORY BEZOBRAZOV
TO HIS SISTER

September 19, 1943

Greetings Vera,

This evening I got a telegram from the High Command in Moscow congratulating me on the high award of Hero of the Soviet Union!

You can well imagine I'm as pleased as punch!

The higher the decoration the harder it is to earn it, that's why I'm doubly gratified. I know I've done some decent scrapping and I'm still putting up a good show to set our Soviet land free. And I shall continue to fight, burn and set fire to the nazis, as befits a hero!

Greetings to all my pals and acquaintances.

Very best wishes to you. Looking forward to a warm welcome home.

Yours,
Grisha

Grigory Bezobrazov was born on January 11, 1919, into a poor peasant family living not far from Kaluga. After secondary school he was accepted into the Krasnodar Air Force Cadet School. In 1940, the young graduate, with the rank of lieutenant, was posted to one of the air units in Byelorussia.

War broke out.... In the arduous years of war, his character matured and will-power steeled battle after battle. His pin-point bombing sent enemy ammunition dumps in the Volga battles into the air, set nazi tanks near the Vistula on fire and smashed fortifications near Berlin. By early 1943, Grigory Bezobrazov had 250-odd sorties to his credit and had dropped thousands of tons of destructive metal onto the heads of the nazis.

Grigory Bezobrazov, Hero of the
Soviet Union

By decree of the Presidium of the Supreme Soviet of the U.S.S.R.,
September 18, 1943, Senior Lieutenant Grigory Bezobrazov was made
Hero of the Soviet Union.

His daring sorties continued to pester the retreating enemy. On
April 18, 1944, the courageous flyer set his bomber on a course for
Berlin. But his plane did not return from its mission. It happened
like this.

On that day Soviet bombers, with their flight commander Bezobrazov
at their head, took off for a bombing raid over one of Berlin's outlying
railway stations, where a large number of soldiers and equipment
were concentrated. The bombers reached its destination without mishap.
Grigory Bezobrazov saw through his bomb sight armoured gun
platforms, hastily covered with a camouflage net, and the tiny, dark
figures of the panicking soldiers. Almost immediately fires flared up
down below, rubble of iron was blown skywards, bombs and ammunition began to explode. It looked as if the tornado of fire started
by the bombs had scorched the very earth under the Germans' feet.

Mission accomplished, the bombers turned for home. But an anti-
aircraft shell had pierced Bezobrazov's plane and it caught fire. Smoke
poured into the cabin and clouded over the instrument panel and
windscreen. It became difficult to observe the ground and the sky.
The crew could hardly breathe. . . .

Grigory Bezobrazov could have bailed out of his burning plane.
But the enemy was waiting below. The Hero of the Soviet Union
took another decision. The bomber, engulfed in flames, dived down
into a cluster of nazi machines.

ALEX. KUZNETSOV'S NOTE
FROM GRANKI DEATH CAMP

Not later than September 22, 1943

Farewell, dear Soviet people. We are to be killed today, but we want to live. We are young, have suffered terrible torture, remained true to our country. . . .

I, Alex. Kuznetsov, Russian, lived in. . . .* My comrade— Valdur Saarestik, from the Estonian S.S.R., Dago Island, hom. . . .*

After the liberation of Smolensk Region, a murder camp was discovered in the village of Granki, in which during two years of bloody slaughter, the occupational forces had shot and tortured many Soviet people. In one of the discovered graves the body of a young lad in a sweater was uncovered. There were no documents on him but in the sleeve of his sweater was concealed a note written on a piece of a German envelope, apparently picked up by the lad somewhere on the road.

* Several words are struck cut.

LETTER
FROM IRINA MALOZHON

Not later than October 1943

Dear Uncle,

I'm not afraid of dying. It's just a pity I've lived so little and done so little for my country. Uncle, I'm already accustomed to the gaol, I'm not the only one, there are many of us. . . . I'm not afraid of dying. Tell mum not to cry. I wouldn't have lived much longer with her anyway. I would have gone my own way. Tell mum to hide the grain, otherwise the Germans will take it. Good-bye.

Yours,
Irina

Up to the war Ukrainian girl Irina Malozhon lived in the village of Zhukli in Chernigov Region.

Like her friends, Irina dreamed of finishing school and going to college. But the war broke out and the girl went to war in defence of her country.

One September day in 1941, a cloud of dust announced the unwelcome arrival of Hitler's tanks and lorryloads of soldiers in the village. A foreign tongue rang out amidst the weeping of women and children thrown out of their cottages by the Germans. The Germans carried off grain, raped, plundered and murdered the peaceful Soviet villagers.

Irina Malozhon joined up with the underground and started to carry out the organisation's instructions. Together with other patriots she printed and distributed leaflets appealing for resistance to the occupational authorities, to their demands for food; they called on the villagers to hide their grain, warm clothing and avoid forced labour. The texts to the leaflets were composed by Irina's uncle Savva Malozhon, to whom Irina's above letter was addressed.

One day, when Irina was passing out leaflets in a neighbouring village, the nazis swooped and the girl was hurled into a dark cellar where she was cruelly tortured. But she stood up to everything. After more suffering in German hands, she was taken out and shot.

LETTER
FROM LIEUTENANT GLUKHOV TO
HIS GIRL-FRIEND

Not later than December 5, 1943

Darling Naya, it's not often I write to you. Not because I don't want to but because I can't write often. You know my life is always in danger. I don't want to give you any vain hopes. I always write to you after a battle. But if you get this letter it means I'm gone, it means I fell in battle with thoughts of you, my faraway yet very near sweetheart.

I took the trouble to write this letter beforehand so that you might know how I loved you, how infinitely dear you were to me.

Just one thing, my dear, sweet Naya, I am not writing this letter to make you wear your heart out in despair and sorrow over me, so that you forever go about in gloom and mourning. No! I'm writing so that you know and remember to the end of your days how much I loved you, how much the very thought of you urged me on, gave me strength in battle, made me scared of nothing when things got really hot.

And there is something else—I want you to know you are a good, decent girl and your love is a haven and oasis for an exhausted soldier.

I have your photo here now before me. Your eyes are looking at me as if they were alive. I see sadness in them. If your picture had been taken with a deliberately affected sorrow, it wouldn't have been so deep and complete as it is in your eyes. I know you've been pining away.

Your letters breathe impatience, you ask me to show no mercy to the nazis so that I come home sooner to you. Believe me—your command, your call—I fulfil with honour. Like you, I live with the dream of returning to you, of being

172

together with you once more. And I know that the farther I go westwards, the quicker my homecoming will be. And for the sake of this dream I rush into battle so ferociously, and manage to do so much that it would amaze even myself if I could read it in a newspaper.

I could get a reprimand if they read this letter, a reprimand for fighting for you. Yet I don't know, I cannot make out, where you end and my country begins. You and she seem to have merged into one for me. And I see your eyes as the eyes of my country. I have the feeling your gaze follows me everywhere, that you, invisible to me, judge my every step.

Your eyes.... When I gaze into them, I get an inexplicable thrill and a quiet contentment. I remember your quick, sly glances. It's only now I appreciate that in those fleeting glances your love came out best and most of all.

You are my future. Why do I talk of the future, though? After all, when you get this letter I shall be no more. I wouldn't like you to receive it, and I won't even write the address on the envelope. But if you do get it, don't take it too much to heart. It just couldn't have been otherwise.

Bye-bye. Be happy without me. You should be able to find yourself a friend and he will be no less happy with you than I was. Cheer up. When V-day comes rejoice and make merry with all the others. Only, when that happy and lucky day comes, I'd like you not to lose that secret, tender grief for me, I'd like your eyes to be suddenly, just for a minute, as they are gazing at me from the picture now.

Please excuse this wish.

All my love and lots of kisses,

Love,
Pyotr

Fighting swirled around an enemy stronghold. In the path of the Soviet soldiers was an enemy bunker from which a hail of machine-gun bullets poured that made it suicide for anyone to even raise their heads. Lieutenant Pyotr Glukhov was hit by a bullet as he was crawling to the gun slit of the bunker a grenade in hand. Some time after, during a lull in the fighting, his battle comrades buried their officer with military honours. Among his personal belongings were found this unsent letter to his girl-friend and her photo. On the back of the photo were the words: "My dear. You are far away but always with me. I am sending you this photo so that you remember me more often. Love to you, my darling. Your Naya. May 1943, Ufa."

173

SERGEANT NAZAROV'S LETTER
TO HIS GIRL-FRIEND

December 5, 1943

Dear Sasha,

Please let my beloved Marusya know I kept my word. I shall fight till my last drop of blood, as she requested.

To me my country is everything—life and love and everything.... Now I see why a Russian cannot be conquered. He loves his country, and there lies his invincibility.

Marusya, we'll soon wipe out the Hitler scum and I'll come home to you.

Dearest Marusya,

We've just crossed the Dnieper, the Germans are attacking. But our lads are holding on!

That's all for now. I'll write again after the battle.

Marusya, love our country like I love her, she will support and save you always and everywhere.

Our country means everything to us.

V. Nazarov

The fighting was hot and furious on the right bank of the Dnieper River. The enemy was putting up dogged resistance and was making counter-attacks time and again. But the Soviet troops held their ground and began to press forward.

On December 5, 1943, Vladimir Nazarov fell during one of these battles. He was always a selfless and fun-loving soldier and had been mentioned for his resolve and efficiency. He was much liked by his fellow soldiers. He began the war as a rifleman and soon distinguished himself as an expert marksman. Once, while fighting off an enemy assault, he put two tanks out of action.

Shortly after, he was made a sniper. When he died he had a total of 168 nazis to his credit.

The story of the above letter is rather interesting. It was written in the heat of the battle on a scrap of paper and handed to a friend, A. Lipatov, with a request to send it to his girl-friend Marusya. Lipatov had no time to ask the girl's surname or her address. Vladimir was killed the same day. In the pocket of his tunic was discovered a photograph of Marusya. On the back of the photo were the words "To my dear Volodya from Marusya Y. 10 V-1943."

Vladimir Nazarov's last wish and letter were published in *Komsomolskaya Pravda* on December 24, 1943.

LIEUTENANT TARASENKO'S
LAST LETTER

December 1943

My dear son Garik,

When you read this letter, many years will have passed, the thunder of war will have died down and a happy and joyful life will once again have blossomed over our liberated land, just as it did before the war. When you were a little boy, you used to lie in your cot and smile through your sleep; mama and I used to think how lucky you were, not having to go through what we had been through in our childhood years. I used to think of bringing you up a real man and was proud of your first words, your first thoughts.

Then came the terrible war and you and mama were evacuated beyond the Volga to save you from death, from the murderers of little children, and I went to defend our country. Probably to you our last meeting in March 1942 in a stranger's hut in Kaisatskaya village was like a dream. You have waited for me a long time and I never came. Like hundreds of thousands of other fathers I died in combat with the cursed foe—the German fascists who invaded our country, broke up our peaceful life, bringing mountains of grief with them.

But, though I die, I am deeply convinced that you, my beloved boy, will live in a free, flourishing country—a country of socialism; you will study in a Soviet school, make your way in life and, like me once upon a time, will learn about the war days from history, read stories about the daring exploits of war heroes. And you, my dear little boy, need not blush for me, for your father, you can proudly say: "My dad died in the fight for future happiness, true to the oath and his country." In a bitter fight with the Germans I shed my blood to gain you the right to a happy life.

Just know this, my beloved son, that my blood too has soaked the soil over which you can walk and build a happy life, about which I dreamed so much.

Years will pass, lots of years, the graves of our enemies will grow over with weeds and thistles while for us defenders our free homeland will build a Victory monument. Remember me when you look at it. Read my letter through and what you don't understand ask your mama, she'll explain.

Put your best foot forward, fight for a better life, and if an enemy ever begins to threaten your beloved homeland, get up and fight and don't let me, your father, down. Don't spare yourself for your homeland.

All my love to you, my dear little son, for all your life, always and ever.

Your loving father,

Grigory Alexeyevich Tarasenko

Grigory Tarasenko was born in 1910 into a worker's family in a village in the Dniepropetrovsk Region. He lost his mother early on (shot by the whiteguards) and from the age of ten had to look after himself.

Thanks to the help of comrades and his own strong will and persistence, he managed to finish a secondary school.

In 1934, he became a schoolmaster in the village of Lyubimovka, Zaporozhye Region.

He gained a commission in the army when war broke out and was seriously wounded in one of the battles on the distant approaches to Rostov-on-Don. After regaining consciousness in the sick bay, Lieutenant Tarasenko asked for a pencil and, with feeble hand, wrote his last letter to his son. The letter, tucked inside his Party card, was kept by nurse A. Khudyakova and passed on to the dead man's son.

Grigory Tarasenko

TESTAMENT OF TANK COMMANDER
JUNIOR LIEUTENANT GEORGI MOROZ

Not later than January 5, 1944

TESTAMENT

I want to leave a brief testament in case I die in battle with the German invaders.

I am a Communist. This small candidate card No. 5902866 and my devotion will carry me on until the invaders are completely routed.

The Bolshevik Party is my leader and inspires me to fresh exploits in battle.

I have been brought up to be a devoted son of my country and the Red Army, a Soviet officer, and everything I gained as a result of hard work in the Syzran Tank School I have put to full use on the field of battle.

I shall fight the enemy until my last drop of blood and my last gasp.

My request to you, my comrades, is to write to my parents after my death and tell them how I fought for my country, how I shot up the nazis and their machines and guns from my tank and how I died.

Please send on my Party card and other documents you find on me to my dear mother and father. Let them have this testament too. May these simple sheets of paper remind them of their son Georgi and how he died during the war.

Their address: Ivan Moroz, Bezymyannaya station, Saratov Region.

Bolshevik greetings to my dear sister Feodosiya—all the best in your studies.

Greetings to my dear comrades Nadezhda Riesman and Valentin Savichev.

Greetings to my college instructors—Captain Zuyev and Sen. Lt. Golyashov and all the others.

Written before the battle,

Jun. Lieutenant G. Moroz

Junior Lieutenant Moroz's tank unit received instructions to disrupt an important enemy transport artery. The tank under his command was the first through enemy lines, but then it was hit and came to a halt. The tank crew continued to shoot down the enemy. When ammunition gave out, Georgi Moroz ordered his crew out of the tank and himself covered their retreat.

Enemy soldiers were creeping up on the tank from all sides. Jun. Lt. Moroz hurled his last grenades. Many nazi soldiers fell but more and more surged on relentlessly towards the lone Soviet tank. Now Moroz had only his pistol. His one thought was to kill as many nazis as he could but to leave one bullet for himself so as not to be taken prisoner.

When his men eventually got through to him they found him dead. In the pocket of his tunic they came across the testament written in ink on a sheet of paper.

Georgi Moroz

CAPTAIN MASLOVSKY'S TESTAMENT
TO HIS SON

January 4, 1944

Well, my dear son, we shan't be seeing each other any more. An hour ago I received orders which mean I shan't be coming back alive. That must be no cause for you to lose heart or be afraid, my lad. Be proud, just as proud as your dad going to his death. I'll do all I can to see you get my letter, and I want you to be careful and not go frightening your grannie.

Glorious Leningrad, the cradle of the revolution, is in danger. Its future may well depend on the successful accomplishment of my mission. For the sake of its safety, I would carry out my mission to my last breath, to my last drop of blood. I could not turn down this mission. Just the opposite, I'm eager to be off, to get down to it as quickly as possible. I'm waiting for the car to take me. A thousand and one thoughts crowd my brain, questions keep flashing through my head like lightning and I answer at once. One of the first questions is: What is the strength that gives me the courage to be a hero? Military discipline and my duty. It's certainly true that there's only one step from discipline to heroism. Remember that, my son, now and forever. And while there's still time, I must take off my decorations and kiss them in the old Guard's tradition. I'm telling you about everything in detail so that you know what sort of man your father was, how and for what he gave his life.

When you grow up, you'll think it over and you will come to love your country. It's a marvellous thing to love your country.

I have a son. My life continues—that's why it's not so hard for me to die. I know that there, deep in the rear, lives and grows the successor to my mind, my heart, my feelings. I go to my death and I see my continuation. My son, in all your letters you begged and expected me to return home from the front. I don't want to deceive you: don't wait any longer and don't grieve, you aren't alone. In the past, my little boy, we haven't had much chance to see each other but I've always loved you and been near to you even though I've often been far away. That's my thought now, even though I'll be dead, my heart will continue to live with you, even death won't take you out of my heart.

In my letter of farewell, I am making a request to my commanding officers to accept my son into the Suvorov Military School, preferably in the Leningrad Region, so that he can visit Poddorsk District, the Sokolsky Village Soviet, because near the village of Khleboyedovo his father met his death.

Good-bye, my son, good-bye, my dearest wife.

Polya, Yura! My wife, my son! You are my dearest love, my own blood, my life! I love you, I love you till my last drop of blood.

Please carry out my last wish.

All my love,

Your ever-loving Gavriil

On a frosty January day in 1944, Captain Gavriil Maslovsky, Chief of Staff of a special skiing battalion, sat in a trench writing his last letter to his son.

The infantry division of the Guards in which he served was holding onto a position not far from the village of Khleboyedovo, Novgorod Region. A scout reported that to the south-east of the neighbouring village of Pryamiki, in the Kruglaya grove, the enemy had a large store of bombs and shells which were about to be dispatched for use against Leningrad. The store had to be destroyed. The divisional commander passed on his instructions to blow up the dump to Captain Maslovsky.

It was already getting dark when Captain Maslovsky finished writing his letter—his last

Gavriil Maslovsky

words to his son Yuri and his wife Polina, who was a surgeon in a field hospital. The brave Communist, a man of iron will, called his letters: "My last written words and wish for my son."

It was almost time to be off.... Captain Maslovsky read the letter through once more. He could imagine his little son Yuri snuggling up in his warm bed and probably wondering: "Where is my dad now?" He so much wanted to see his son, caress his curly head, press him to his breast. But the rules of war are inexorable, it was time to go.... A few hours later a column of flame shot into the dark sky and the earth trembled from a big explosion. The job had been done, but Captain Maslovsky never returned.

His comrades sent the letter to his son Yuri, who, true to his father's last wish, graduated in 1952 from the Sverdlovsk Suvorov School and then a military motor and tractor college, and became a Soviet Army officer.

Cavalli Maslovsky

PASHA SAVELYEVA'S INSCRIPTION
ON THE WALL OF A DEATH CELL IN LUTSK

January 1944

The awful, horrible minute is approaching! My whole body is mutilated—I've practically no hands, no legs.... But I die without uttering a sound. It's terrible to die at 22. How I want to live! We depart for the sake of those coming after us, for your sake, my country.... Blossom, be beautiful, my native land, and farewell. Your Pasha.

Pasha Savelyeva was born into a peasant family and went to school in the town of Rzhev. In the summer of 1940, after graduating from the Moscow College of Finance and Economics, she went to work in Lutsk. She was there when war broke out. Failing to evacuate to the east, she decided to fight the occupational forces in the town. After a while, she formed an underground group with other young people. The courageous underground fighters gathered information about the location of Hitler's troops, engaged in sabotage, assisted in the escape of Soviet prisoners and supplied them with documents and clothing. In early summer 1943, the group managed to establish contact with the partisans operating somewhere near under the command of D. Medvedev, Hero of the Soviet Union.

They got their hands on the nazi plan of Lutsk with all the military objectives clearly marked. On instructions from the partisan centre, they caused the Germans a lot of trouble on the railway. The nazis were run off their feet trying to discover the people behind the underground resistance.

On December 22, 1943, the Gestapo made a late call on Pasha Savelyeva. After horrible torture and suffering, the nazis burned the young patriot in January 1944 in the courtyard of an old, medieval Catholic church, which the Germans had turned into a large torture chamber.

An hour before execution she managed to pass the following note to the cell next to her: "If they bring us out together let's try and make a break for it. Perk up!" But they had no chance.

She scratched the above inscription with a nail on her cell wall just a few minutes before she was executed.

GUNNER VADIM USOV'S
BATTLE PLEDGE

February 20, 1944

As I go into battle, I swear to do my sacred duty for my homeland and put all my hatred into my fighting skill—it will treble my strength!

Even when I'm gone, my feat of arms will not be forgotten. I would have liked to have lived but I have to sacrifice myself so that my happy country may live and prosper, so that others may live.

My dear country, accept my modest gift for your good, and remember that I, brought up, fed and reared by you, have repaid you with everything I had.

I, your son, was devoted to you right up to my dying days and I have carried out my duty as a Communist and soldier with a pure heart.

I have died so that you may live. I loved you fervently, my homeland, and I hated your enemies.

... The final salvoes will die away and the dark war clouds will disperse to reveal a free homeland, a free nation. And whoever of you will live to see that great victory day, that clear and joyful day, remember and pass on the story of those who did not spare themselves to bring that day, who gave their lives for it, to bring our triumph near.

You know, I, too, wanted to be with you on that day.

On that day I want you, Natasha dear, to remember the man who used to live for you and, dying, used to think of you, my unforgettable sweetheart.

Dearest mother, Lyalechka, Pavlik and Lyonechka, don't grieve and weep for me, lighten your grief with the thought that I was true to my duty to the very end, to my soldier's job and shed my blood to hasten victory day.

Dear friends, I ask you for the last time to let my comrades-in-arms know about this pledge. Then send it to my family and write about me to Natalya Sergeyevna Ivanova, born 1927, living at 1/4 Sovietsky Lane, Anzhero-Sudzhensk, Kemerovo Region.

My mother's address: Valentina Nikolayevna Usova, Lednevo State Farm, Nebylovsky District, Ivanovo Region.

Vadim Usov was born on November 24, 1923. In 1941, he finished secondary school in Leningrad and gained admission to the Dzerzhinsky Higher Naval-Engineering College. His dream was to study and join the Navy.

At the end of 1941, he was sent with other cadets to the front. Right from the start the young cadet scorned death and fought where the fighting was at its hottest. He became a battle-hardened N.C.O. in no time. His comrades liked him for his modesty and his fearlessness, for his sensitive, kind heart.

He fought his last battle on February 20, 1944, in Karelia. From a bunker on a hill, the nazis had raked with fire just about every foot of ground and it would have been risking mass suicide for the Soviet men to have attempted an assault of the hill. Then the unit commander ordered Vadim Usov, a gun crew commander, to push his gun as close as possible to the bunker and blast it wide open. It took Vadim's crew eight shells to set the bunker on fire. But by this time enemy shells from two gun batteries fell so thick and fast around Usov's field piece that it was a miracle they did not make a direct hit. Vadim Usov gave the order for his men to take cover in the trenches while he made a dash for his gun. But a shell got there first and he was killed by shrapnel.

When the battle was over, Vadim's comrades found his "Battle Pledge" among his documents.

Vadim Usov

LETTERS
FROM TANK COMMANDER VADIM SIVKOV
AND WIRELESS-OPERATOR PYOTR KRESTYANINOV

SIVKOV'S AND KRESTYANINOV'S LETTER TO
THEIR COMRADES

We two remain alone in tank No. 17–tank commander Jun. Lt. Vadim Sivkov and wireless-operator Pyotr Krestyaninov. We prefer death in our own tank than to desert it.

We will not be taken prisoner, so we are leaving 2 or 3 bullets each for ourselves. Blame for the accident must be put on our driver who did not carry out my orders and turn to the left. When he jumped out I didn't shoot him for fear of blocking the escape hatch.

Twice the Germans have approached the tank but haven't been able to open the hatches. In our last minute of life we shall blow up the tank with grenades so that the enemy doesn't get hold of it. Please tell our people at home that we did our duty to our country by capturing Yavkino with only one tank, and then dying there.

Address: Lieutenant-Colonel Sivkov, District Military Committee, Karakulino, Udmurt A.S.S.R.

Konstantin Krestyaninov, Ralniki, Shurminsky District, Kirov Region.

Sivkov
P. Krestyaninov

March 15, 1944, 6.10 a.m.

My Dear Dad, Mum and Tasenka,

Just to let you know I've only been at the front a little over a month. We've covered more than sixty miles in our advance. On March 13, with a single tank I captured the large village of Yavkino (1,167 homesteads according to the 1930 map). On the night of March 15, the Germans counter-attacked and recaptured the village. In the dark my tank ran into an anti-tank trench. Just the two of us, my wireless-operator and myself, are left. We decided to die if necessary, but we shan't surrender. Two or three times the Germans have come up to the tank but they haven't got it open yet. It looks like these are the last minutes of my life. That, in brief, is about all. Don't worry about me. That's war for you. All the best for your future happiness. My last request: let the boys in Izhevsk know about my death. Well, that's about all.

Good-bye forever,

Your son,

Vadim

Sivkov

March 15, 1944, 7 a.m.

It was the morning of March 13, 1944. The Soviet Army was beating back the nazis from Russian soil. Among the leading units was the 212th Separate Tank Regiment. Tank No. 17 of this regiment pushed on ahead, mercilessly pursuing and mowing down the fleeing enemy. Skilfully manoeuvring over the rugged terrain, the tank came out to the village of Yavkino and ran into a strong barrage of fire from the Germans entrenched in the village. The tank crew, led by Junior Lieutenant Sivkov, decided to surge forward and drive the nazis out of the village. Moving right up to the edge of the village the tank opened up with all guns blazing, and at top speed tore into the village. Diving and ditching among the houses, the tank made it appear that at least a dozen tanks had burst into the village. The nazis dashed out from houses, along the streets into the gardens, but could not escape the Soviet tank's relentless fire. By mid-day no enemy soldiers remained. And it was not long before the village was completely taken over by the forward infantry detachments of the Soviet Army.

According to an incomplete count, it was estimated that as a result of the tank crew's daring action, some 250 Germans had been killed and more than 100 different carts destroyed. Among the trophies were 3 tanks in good shape, 12 armoured carriers, 3 guns, 5 mortars, 75 lorries and 250 carts.

Two days passed. The foe, having summoned up his reserves, rushed into the counter-attack. Wave after wave of Germans converged on Yavkino. And once again the tank, swerving through the village, stopped the enemy's advance. But it ran into bad luck. As it sharply rounded a house the tank pitched into an anti-tank trench. The cannon, rammed into the trench wall, was silenced.

The nazis filtered back into the village and surrounded the stranded tank. But there were Soviet men inside the tank—tank commander Junior Lieutenant Vadim Sivkov and wireless operator Pyotr Krestyaninov. And when Hitler's men hammered on the armoured sides shouting "Russ, surrender!", the only answer they got was a firm: "Russians do not surrender."

The tank men were Y.C.L. members, both born in 1925. They had met up in the 212th Separate Tank Regiment. And for near on two months they had been fighting shoulder to shoulder on the 3rd Ukrainian Front.

When their tank had blundered into the pit they both understood there was no way out. They checked their pistols and piled up their remaining hand grenades. Even before the two friends had finished writing their farewell letters home, they heard the nazis clamouring on the tank's side. Seeing they would not be able to take the tank men alive, the Germans dragged up the artillery piece to blast the tank open. But the Soviet pair beat them to it. There was a tremendous explosion and on the spot where the tank had stood a sheet of flame shot up engulfing the enemy soldiers around.

Two days later Soviet units once more recaptured the village. The remnants of the two tank men were buried with full military honours. A short while after, a soldier on his way through the village spotted the tank and on investigation, pulled a charred iron box from the wreckage. Inside the box were two sheets of paper—the farewell letters of the two heroes.

On May 24, 1944, a decree of the Presidium of the Supreme Soviet of the U.S.S.R. was published awarding the two brave men the titles of Hero of the Soviet Union.

NOTE AND INSCRIPTION
BY TANK COMMANDER ALEXANDER DEGTYAREV

INSCRIPTION ON Y.C.L. CARD

I die a courageous death for my country's liberation.
March 22, 1944.

NOTE ON WRITING PAD

Please write about my death at the front to my parents at the following address: Nikolai Degtyarev, Flat 9, Block 3, 151 Bolshaya Sadovaya, Saratov; and to my bride, Adelaida Pulina, 4 Aptechnaya St., Saratov.

Tank commander Lieutenant Alexander Degtyarev was among the advancing troops that were beating back the Germans to the west. In the streets of Chertkov he engaged enemy tanks. Lieutenant Degtyarev's tank knocked out a Tiger and an armoured carrier, but at that moment an enemy 105-millimetre gun fired from an ambush and knocked off the tank's turret. The driver carried his wounded commander to the nearest house and himself ran for aid. Sensing his end was near, Alexander Degtyarev pulled out his Y.C.L. card and pad and wrote his last words to his comrades with a wounded hand.

WALL INSCRIPTIONS IN TIRASPOL GESTAPO CELLS

Partisan Popik Demyan from cell 46 was shot on October 14, 1943, at 9 p.m.
11.XII.43, 18 partisans shot from cell 32.

Alexander Kozlov–Soviet paratrooper–landed in the vicinity of Breulov, arrested 20.XII.43. Petropavlovsky miners' settlement, Karpinsky District, Sverdlovsk Region. Alexander Kozlov died 7.II.44.
Glory to him, eternal glory!
In the hearts of patriots and all honest people
He will not die, but live forever.
The country will not forget him.

Brothers, avenge our blood, the blood of paratrooper Alexander Kozlov. Get revenge on the nazis. Show no mercy. We know our men will come and read these words.

Vasya Buzhenko died here, 10 Proletarskaya St., Ananyev, Odessa Region. Good-bye Mum, Dad and brother Kolechka. Your son Vasya Buzhenko. Love to you all, 3rd April, 44.

Don't despair, we shall win because we stand firm. May hope for victory be your guiding star in minutes of despair. Don't lose hope.

The whole world is fighting for justice, for our life. We'll win because we have the Communist Party behind us.

Keep up your spirits even in this cess-pit. Victory is ours. 29.III.1944, at 10.30 p.m. wonderful news—we've won.
Workers of the world, unite!

The Moldavian Republic was liberated after ringing off and wiping out a very large concentration of enemy forces around Kishinev and Jassy. At the end of August 1944, troops of the 3rd Ukrainian Front brought freedom to the Moldavian people. On August 27, the last shots resounded on the eastern bank of the Prut River.

At every step Soviet soldiers came upon evidence of the abominable crimes of Hitler's men. The monsters had tortured and murdered tens of thousands of Soviet people here. In April of 1944 alone, the nazis in Tiraspol shot over 2,000 men and women.

These inscriptions were made on walls, plank beds and doors of cell 46—the death cell—in the First Gestapo Gaol and in the cells of Tiraspol's Second Gaol. These cells once held Soviet patriots condemned to be shot. Most of the inscriptions were made in Russian, some in Rumanian, and a few reproduced in English and French.

WALL INSCRIPTIONS
IN TALLINN GESTAPO GAOL

May 1942 to April 1944

CELL NO. 5

Good-bye, all my comrades. I'll see you no more.

Pyotr Kornyev

Long live the U.S.S.R.! Ivan Timofeyevich Kuleshov.
22.IV.–44.

CELL NO. 7

Long live the Estonian S.S.R. Death for death.
Boichenko Y. 2/5–42.
Workers of the world, unite! Our cause is just, the foe
will be smashed, victory will be ours!

CELL NO. 19

Vladimir Lositsky was here, 1910, Golibisov village,
Starodubsky District, Orel Region. Sentenced to be shot
in 1943, X. 27. Please let my parents know at the above
address–Alexander Lositsky. Farewell, dear friends and my
country. Farewell, my children, they are taking me out to
be shot.
Good-bye forever.*

---

* This inscription was made on the back of the bedside stand.

Farewell, friends!

Sentenced to be shot 1/XII-43 imprisoned officer from 92 Infantry Division, 317 Infantry Regiment, Volkhov Front, 23 Strike Force. Taken prisoner wounded 25/VI-42. Was in Pskov camp. Arrested 26/III-43. 24/VII—Pskov, gaol, cell 12. From 25/VII-43 Revel Gaol, cell 40 and from 1/XII-43—solitary 1/17.

These inscriptions were made in Tallinn Gestapo gaols. On investigation of the gaol buildings shortly after the town's liberation by the Soviet Army, a number of inscriptions on cell walls, beds and tables were discovered. They had been made by former inmates doomed by the German occupational forces. Some of the inscriptions are reproduced above.

LETTERS
FROM RIGA UNDERGROUND LEADER
IMANT SUDMALIS TO HIS WIFE AND CHILDREN

6 Upmalas St., Liepaya. To be sent after the war.

IV. 1944

Marusenka,

Hardly likely that you will receive this, my last letter, but you might all the same!

On April 13, I was sentenced to death, I don't know the date today, the days are all mixed up. But a lot of time has passed since the trial, it must be about April 28 and I'm thinking that it may well be our little Aijuk's birthday today—six years old now—and maybe I shall be taken out to be shot tonight.

They don't give me any books, I'm alone in the empty, solitary central prison, I've got plenty of time to think over the past. I look back to the past and see what a terrific amount we've been through in these short years, I recollect many wonderful minutes. And these memories of the tight spots I've been in, of the peaceful, sunny hours with you—these memories help me now. I don't regret the path I have come....

There could be so much to say and write about but I have no pencil—I found a tiny piece of chipped lead in my pocket and I'm writing with that.

You'll probably never know what fence I'll be buried under, it doesn't really matter much—the same old earth will cover us all. I have an idea, my love, that after the war you'll go back to our dear Latvia. And there, sometime in the evening after your day's work, remember that once upon a time there was a man named Imis who loved you—tell Aijuk and Sarmuk something about him.

Bring our laddies up the right way, Marusenka, teach them to love the future in which they will live and for which so much blood has been shed.

Give Aijuk and Sarmuk a caress for me, good-bye Marusenka, we'll see each other no more. Don't want to die yet, but believe me—I know how to die in the proper way. The Gadfly, too, was shot in the spring when the young grass was pushing through. Look after yourself and try to be happy, Marusenka. Don't take it too badly.

Your Imis

May 25, 1944

Dear Marusenka, Aijuk, Sarmuk,

Can't tell whether you'll ever read my final words, but I'm writing anyway. In a couple of hours I'll be executed. The trial was on 13th May,* so I've had a fair amount of time to ponder over my life. When I look back over the days gone by, I have nothing to reproach myself for. I acted like a man and a real fighter in those fateful days.

If only the future is lovely and happy, it certainly should be! All that blood surely cannot have been shed in vain.

Don't drown yourself in sorrow, my Marusenka, no one has yet ever lived eternally. Bring up Aijuk and Sarmuk so that they remember me sometimes, so that their lives are happier and better.

Look after yourself, Marusenka, thanks for all the good you gave me. And please give Aijuk and Sarmuk a hug for me.

Imis

Imant Sudmalis was a Latvian partisan, the brains behind the Riga resistance movement.

As secretary of the Liepaya District Y.C.L. Committee and member of the Central Committee of the Latvian Communist Party, he immediately took his stand in the front ranks of the fight against the nazi invaders. On the second day of war, the Liepaya young people formed a rifle company headed by Imant Sudmalis and Boris Pelnen, secretary of the Liepaya Y.C.L. Committee. Liepaya workers' detachments and Soviet soldiers and sailors who made up the small gar-

---

* The trial was, in fact, on 13th of April.

Imant Sudmalis

rison in the town put up a staunch resistance for five days. Imant Sudmalis turned out to be an excellent machine-gunner and daring commander. After the fall of Liepaya he headed a group of young fighters who broke through the besieged port area and went underground in Kurzeme.

After a few months in Kurzeme, Imant Sudmalis made his way back to Riga where he set about establishing an underground organisation. In the spring of 1942, a decision was taken to send him across the front to report on the results of resistance work and receive fresh instructions. He set off in May of the same year. He met up with Alexander Grom's partisan group then operating in the Byelorussian forests. They helped him to cross the front line and by autumn he was in Moscow.

In November, a Latvian partisan detachment was formed in the Soviet rear. Imant Sudmalis was appointed Party organiser. At the beginning of December, when the Russian winter was at its worse, the detachment crossed the front at a point called Velikiye Luki and made a 200-mile incursion into the Kalinin Region eventually setting up a base in a forest in Byelorussia on the border with Latvia. From December 1942 to January 1943, the detachment succeeded in uniting the Ludzen and Daugavpils partisan groups operating along the border. By its actions, the detachment created a base for future activity of the Operative Group of the Central Committee of the Latvian Communist Party—the organisational headquarters for the underground movement in Latvia. On March 22, 1943, a Latvian partisan brigade was formed on the basis of this detachment.

On July 20, 1943, Imant Sudmalis, on the authorisation of the Latvian Y.C.L. Central Committee, returned to Riga where he became head of the underground groups, directing and extending their activities. He established contacts between the Riga underground and the partisan units in North Latvia, and took part in many dangerous operations. The most outstanding of them was the foiling of the "Latvian People's Protest Meeting" which the Germans had intended to stage in connection with the work of the Moscow Conference of the Allies, which had discussed questions concerning the Baltic area. The meeting was due to be held on November 13, 1943, on Riga's Domskaya Square. Reichskommissar Loze, one of Hitler's top-ranking officers, was billed to address the meeting. At 10 in the morning a bomb exploded on Domskaya Square which the resistance men had planted under the platform. The meeting's organisers took to their heels. Utilising the ensuing hubbub, the crowd evaded the police cordon and scattered. The nazis put up a sum of 30,000 imperial marks for the head of the man responsible for the explosion. But Imant was elusive. In December he was responsible for the starting up of an underground print-shop in Riga.

The Gestapo did all they could to wipe out the Riga underground organisation. In February 1944, mass arrests began. Sensing that a provocateur had penetrated the resistance, Imant Sudmalis ordered the abandonment of all the old secret apartment hide-outs, disbanded the underground groups and dispatched all possible underground suspects to the partisans. The complete destruction of the underground was staved off but Imant himself was seized by the nazis and on May 25, 1944, at 6 o'clock in the evening, was hanged in the cell of the fifth block of the Riga prison.

Imant Sudmalis was posthumously awarded the title of Hero of the Soviet Union.

His letters, written in Latvian to his wife Maria, were discovered after the war in a crack in the wall of his death cell.

VOLODYA USTRITSOV'S NOTE
FROM A NAZI GAOL IN PESHIN

May 26, 1944

Long live the U.S.S.R.–Russia!
Here from 6 to 26-5-44.
Please inform: 19 Syezdovskaya, Vasilyevsky Island, Lenin-
grad 53–Volodya Ustritsov, Y.C.L. member, sailor, sentenced
to death 20-IV-1944. Shot 26-V-44.
For the Party!

Volodya Ustritsov, wounded and taken prisoner, bravely endured
all the nazi torture. On May 6, 1944, the retreating nazis transferred
him to Peshin gaol in Poland and killed him on May 26. Before
dying he scratched a few parting words with a nail on a piece of
black cardboard. After the town's liberation, Polish security officials
came across the cardboard in the Gestapo archives and sent it to the
Soviet Union.

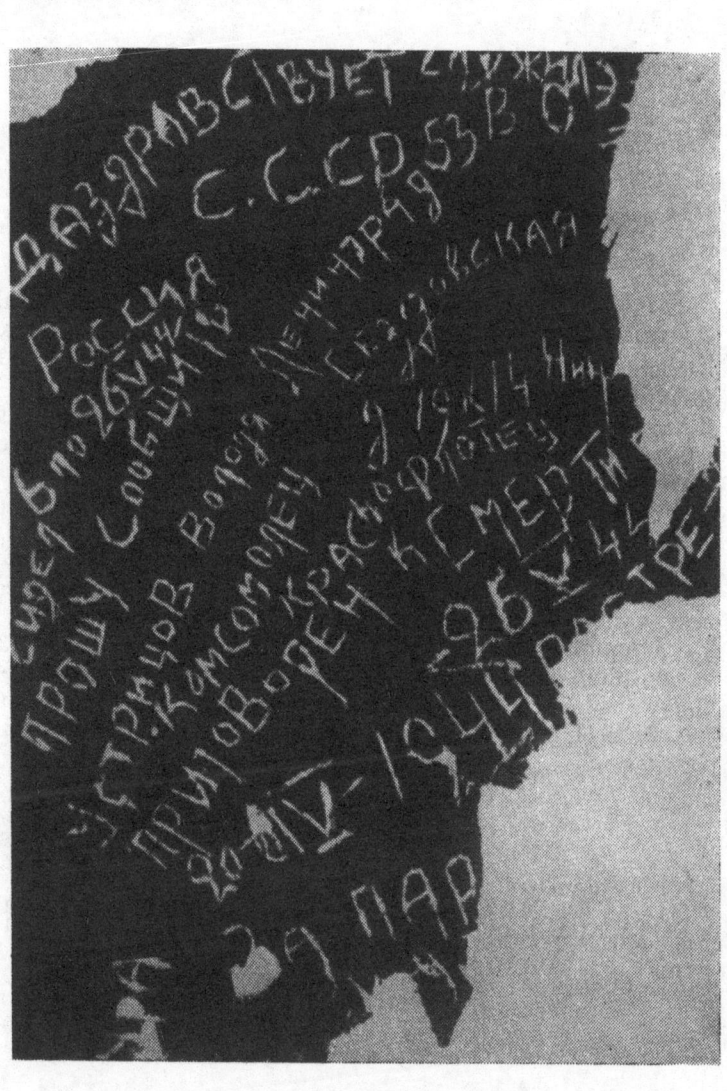

EXCERPTS FROM NOTEBOOK
OF ARTILLERY OFFICER IVAN ALEXEYEV

I am defending a very valuable, important and crucial district. It really is something to defend. Vital highways. Though the place is dangerous, we cannot abandon it. If I die, it will be worth it.

Glory to the late Junior Lieutenant V. M. Shchekin. His name will live forever in my heart as my best man. He fought for his country to his final breath.

30–05–44

After my death, please send my decorations to my grey-haired father. Let him know my words.

"Your son Vanya carried out his father's advice and behest without begrudging any strength or even his life.

"Accomplished well. With my unit, I brought down 23 enemy planes. July 6, 1941, in the region of Troni (Bessarabia) we wiped out over a battalion of infantrymen and on July 8, 1941, beat off 12 tanks, burned one tank, others sent packing."

Vanya Alexeyev

Ivan Alexeyev went to the front straight from college. Put in command of a gun battery, he bravely fought the enemy. The young Chuvash was much respected and liked in the army. He was killed on June 13, 1944.

LETTERS FROM SIGNALMAN
OLEG NECHITOVSKY

May 1944

LETTER TO HIS MOTHER

Good-bye, my dear Mother,

This is my dying letter and if you ever get it you will know that your son is gone. I died as your son and as the son of my country. I didn't spare my life for people's good and happiness, for your peaceful old age, for a happy life for the children.

No tears! Be proud and don't forget me. Please tell the young ones that you once had a son and that he didn't spare himself and gave his life for their future and their happiness.

I find it terribly hard to write you this letter but I am firmly convinced my comrades will carry on where I left off. The nazis will be wiped off the face of the earth, and they won't get any peace in the other world either. I am Ukrainian, but Byelorussian soil will take me as her son just as well.

All my love and kisses to you for the last time!

Your son Oleg

Whoever finds this letter, please send it to: Yevgeniya Nechitovskaya, Flat 6, 144 Prozorovskaya St., Kiev.

LETTER TO HIS GIRL-FRIEND

Farewell, my darling Lidushka,

This is my last letter. And if you ever get it, I shall no longer be alive. Please understand that I gave my life dearly, honourably, on the battlefield, and the Byelorussian soil has accepted me, son of the Ukraine, as her own son.

It's no use crying, better spare a thought for me now and again, be proud that the man who loved you, who wanted to build a life together with you, died honourably for his country, for people's happiness. Of course I didn't want to die, but the call of our country is law, my duty called and life had to take second place.

We dreamed of so much, but. ... The years will pass, you will have a son and I would like you to tell him just a tiny bit about the man who wanted to be his father.

That's all, good-bye,

Love and lots of kisses for the last time!

Your loving Oleg

Whoever finds this letter, please send it to: Lapidus (for Lida Abalyshnikova), Flat 6, 25 Engels St., Kharkov.

At the beginning of 1944, the Soviet Army were beating back the nazis westwards on all fronts. By May the troops of the 1st Byelorussian Front were fighting on the right bank of the River Dnieper and clearing the Polessye Region from the nazis.

During the battles for Big and Small Kalinkovichi, the commander of the forward battalion lost contact with the company operating ahead in the region of the main thrust. Things began to look desperate for the stranded men. It was vital to re-establish contact at all cost. Signalman Oleg Nechitovsky was called upon to perform the extremely dangerous mission.

He realised that he was going to an almost certain death, since the area where the cable had been damaged was constantly under fire. He searched for and found the break in the line with shells bursting all around him. Wounded and fast losing blood, he never stopped work splicing the broken line. His last words sent along the repaired line were: "Order accomplished. Line's back to normal." Sensing that he could not muster enough strength to crawl back, he wrote his last letters to his mother and girl-friend.

When the enemy retreated, his comrades found him already cold. The two letters were discovered in his pocket.

Oleg Nechitovsky

ALEXANDER MOKSHIN'S NOTE

June 1944

I swear to spare neither blood nor my life fighting for the complete liberation of our beautiful country!

In the summer of 1944, sailors of the Ladoga Fleet took part in the offensive on the Karelian Front, backing up the soldiers on shore from the left flank. Particularly vital were the Tuloksin landings whereby the sailors forced a bridgehead in the enemy rear between the Olontsa and Vidlitsa rivers and straddled the railway and road routes.

Alexander Mokshin from a landing party scouting out the district around the village of Vidlitsa found himself up against a strong covering detachment. There was no escape. Alone against a whole platoon of nazis he fired his submachine-gun and hurled hand grenades. Eleven nazis were killed, but the enemy was closing in. So as not to fall into their hands, Alexander Mokshin reserved his last hand grenade for himself.

After the village's capture, his comrades found the small note and vow written on his Party card.

INSCRIPTIONS
IN THE LAMSDORF PRISON CAMP

ON CELL DOOR NO. 8

Better death than nazi prison!
Master escaper Lisitsa Ivan G. was here imprisoned 3.9.43.

ON CELL DOOR NO. 14

Kazakh Kolya Zhakulbekov (Dotsent*), sentenced to be shot for political work, was here. Formerly Sen. Lt. tank man, recently arrived from Lublin, awaiting death.
Farewell, light of day!
Farewell, my native land!

Kolya, 15/VII–44

During the occupation of Poland, a large number of concentration camps were formed on her territory holding many civilians and Soviet p.o.w.s.

When the Soviet Army liberated the Lamsdorf camp in Poland they found dozens of inscriptions on barrack walls, prison beds and cell doors, made by Soviet patriots awaiting death. These inscriptions are documentary proof of the invincible will of Soviet people who preserved their human dignity in the face of nazi abominations.

---

* Probably a nickname.

LETTER
FROM RIGA UNDERGROUND FIGHTER
HADO LAPSA
WITH POSTSCRIPT BY EDUARDS INDULEN
FROM THE CENTRAL RIGA GAOL

August 26, 1944

Approx. 10 p.m.

Dear Sis,

You will probably be surprised at my wanting to write when you get this long letter from Pyotr. But there we are—before they pump 8 grams of lead into me today, I want to get off my chest everything that has heaped up there over the past couple of months. In this letter I shan't write about myself but about the unfortunate comrades who have been with me. So as well as avenging me, I want you all to avenge the inhuman suffering of these poor devils a hundredfold and give them some measure of satisfaction. I don't know whether I shall be able to put it over to you but I am going to try. I have seen mutilated corpses dug up after they have lain in the ground for several months. Before that I never imagined I would ever have to see live people in such a condition here, in Riga, in the cellars on Reimers Street.* Damn that blasted house with all its inhabitants—the German murderers and their obedient, sadistic henchmen and the other dirty swine.

I was arrested on June 2, 1944. On that day I was put into a cellar of this frightful house. I was in the first cell which contained 7 or 8 inmates including the blacksmith

___

* In Riga's Reimers St. (now Communard St.) the Gestapo had their H.Q.

Klyava, or Klyavin, as far as I can remember, from Ogra Volost. At the beginning, I paid no attention to anyone being so taken up with my own worries. In a couple of hours I calmed down and began to chat with my companions-in-misfortune. Each of them spoke of his own troubles and showed signs of torture on his body. It was a terrible sight but I could hardly believe my eyes when, after some hesitation, Klyava, a pale-faced fellow, somewhere between 40 and 45 who sat all the while to one side, pulled off his shirt with an almost expressionless face. What we then saw was no longer a human body. His entire body, from head to toe, was unlike all the others—blue or all colours of the rainbow—it looked like the poor man had been roasted alive—his whole body was swollen and a dark brown colour.

Blacksmith Klyava told us about himself—he was married, father of two children and from 1940-41 had been an active trade union worker. When the Germans came, he was arrested for his union activities but after some neighbours had vouched for him was set free. He was taken in for the second time at the end of June and delivered to the Ogra S.D. police. It was there that he had been worked over. A coward of an informer had accused him of sympathy with the Bolsheviks and of keeping a revolver. For this non-existent weapon the Latvian police had beaten him up for six days on end. The first day had been awful, the second even worse, but after that he felt no more pain.

Most of the time the German murderers had always been drunk. They "worked" in turns of three until the victim lost consciousness. When he passed out they waited until he came to and the "work" continued. As I said before, this continued for six days. Then Klyava was taken to Riga. They also arrested his wife. What happened to her and the children he, of course, hadn't the faintest idea. I saw this unfortunate man three or four times when he was taken in for questioning. They lashed into him here too; the nazis' "law" is based on one thing only—inhuman use of power.

The last time I saw Klyava after interrogation I didn't know what to do. I was horrified and speechless with impotent rage. A few hours later he was brought down to our cell. He was no longer a human being, but a martyr taken down from the wrack. If his cell-mates hadn't supported him and sat him on a bench next to the radiator which he used for cooling his battered face, he would have fallen. The martyr was only semi-conscious—his face was beaten to pulp, his left ear partly ripped off, his bloody face was swollen and as pale as a dead man's, except for the marks left by the beating. I had never cried before, but when I saw him I felt the tears welling in my eyes.

From then on, I had only one desire—that he and the others, like Ludvig and Malvina Kukurevič, murdered on August 8, should be avenged. I could still tell you plenty more, my sweet sister, but my time is running out—at any moment they will be taking me to Bikerniek Forest.*

Sis, you always were a real Soviet woman, and your duty is to do all you can so that as soon as this rotten system collapses, the names of these unfortunate martyrs, which can be read on the walls of the Central Gaol's second cell, shall be the accusers of these blasted nazis and even more hateful Latvian quislings.

All these curs must get their deserts. Nobody must forget the words of P. Ozol at his trial—that he was beaten with a riding crop, with a stool, that they stamped on him, and three days after the interrogation he was still giving out blood instead of urine.

These savages can never be pardoned for feeding people only on boiled water with a bit of flour until they dropped from hunger and exhaustion, as happened with me.

Don't forget, you who remain alive, that we were clubbed across the face for the slightest thing and threatened to be shot. We suffered this horror every night, holding our breath and waiting to be taken to the scaffold or to Bikerniek Forest. We heard the groans and screams of our comrades as they were being carted away. We saw a battered man brought back from interrogation who died within half an hour without regaining consciousness. (It happened in cell 26 in the first block. My comrades Andrejs Grauds and M. Klanis are witnesses.) Death to the bloody S.D. curs and the lackeys of the German fascists.

I hope you won't doubt the integrity of this short letter. Everything written here pales terribly in comparison with reality, but, as I've already said, time is very short.

---

* Place where mass shooting took place outside Riga.

I don't know if I'll be able to write to the end of this page. Therefore please fulfil my only wish. Going to my death I'm deeply convinced that I and my last cell-mate Indulen and the many murdered and tortured fighters will be worthily avenged and our relatives contented. But I wish that when Latvia is again free and you receive this letter, it will be published and those who survive will learn how thousands of us died.

Once more I beg you—don't grieve over me and don't shed any tears, for I die for my convictions, in the knowledge that I did a lot to destroy the country of slaves—Germany—and will ever remain in the memory of all my comrades as a man who was not afraid of either truth or death.

Your brother Hado

Greetings to everyone from Inda who is always in good spirits and will go to his death with a smile.

E. Indulen

Hado Lapsa and Eduards Indulen were leading members of the Latvian underground. Under their leadership, documents and passports were prepared for members of the anti-fascist organisations in Riga. On June 2, 1944, Hado Lapsa was arrested. Shortly after Eduards Indulen also fell into the hands of the Gestapo. In the morning of August 27, 1944, the two Soviet patriots were shot by the Riga Gestapo.

NIKOLAI SUCHKOV'S NOTE

Not later than September 9, 1944

I gave my life for our Communist Party, for our glorious Komsomol, which brought me up.

Please, comrades, get this slip of paper to the Y.C.L. organiser in our battalion. Let him know a Y.C.L. man doesn't let his side down in battle.

This note was discovered on a dead Red Army man, Nikolai Suchkov, after a furious skirmish with nazi submachine-gunners. Eighteen-year-old Nikolai Suchkov surged forward in the heat of battle and found himself surrounded by Germans. He had no hand grenades and his ammunition had almost run out. Realising he would not escape the nazis alive, he quickly scribbled a few words on a scrap of paper.

POEMS AND NOTES
LEFT BY TATAR POET MUSA JALIL

1943-44

True to its pledge is my heart to the last,
When doom overcasts my brow.
It was songs I gave to my land in the past;
'Tis my life I must give her now.
Singing, I welcomed the fragrance of spring,
Singing, I fought and bled.
Today the last of my songs I sing:
The axe hangs over my head.
It was songs that taught me freedom to prize,
Now they bid me to die as a Fighter.
My life was a love-song that soared to the skies,
Let my death be the battle-song of a fighter.

TO A FRIEND

Friend, do not grieve that we depart so soon.
Death lies in store for everyone on earth.
Man lay the limits of his years himself.
But years are not the yardstick of life's worth,
Nor is the time between one's birth and death
A credit worthy measure of its length.
Blood spilled in the defence of a just cause
Brings heroes deathlessness, their cause—immortal
strength.

October 1943

HEROISM

Your song breathes fire, your song breathes love
For your native land—what more?
Nay, soldiers are not famed for songs,
But for their deeds at war.
      Say, poet, did you rise and fight
      When the hour of battle came?
      In crucial times that try men's souls
      The bold alone win fame.
To fight and win, to crush the foe,
One must be firm and brave.
Courage alone brings liberty.
The coward stays a slave.
      Entreaties are of no avail
      When men succumb to chains.
      But he who fights with sword in hand
      Forever free remains.
What worth is there in life enthralled,
What happiness in gaol?
Life's beauty lies in liberty,
All joys before it pale.
      Your name lives on when you give your
                        life
      To free familiar parts.
      The traitor's blood is mixed with mud,
      The hero's fires men's hearts.
The hero, dying, does not die.
His fame survives his death.
Then fight and glorify your name,
Fight, whilst you draw your breath!

                                 December 1943

LAST WORDS

Bluish-grey and snow-bound streets.
Blizzards blow their last.
Three guards with automatic guns
Lead their victim past,
      Past houses veiled with falling snow,
      Through the silent night.
      And there, behind their snow-cloaked
                       backs
      Spring burgeons, fair and bright.

Bluish-grey and snow-bound streets.
Blizzards blow their last.
Three guards are levelling their guns.
Their victim's days are past.

JALIL'S TESTAMENT WRITTEN ON BACK COVER OF HIS FIRST NOTEBOOK

December 1943

To the friend who can understand Tatar and will read this notebook.

It was written by the Tatar people's poet Musa Jalil. After suffering all the horrors of a nazi prison camp without yielding to the fear of the forty deaths, he was taken to Berlin. Here he was accused of being involved in an underground organisation and the distribution of Soviet propaganda... and put in prison. He will be sentenced to death and die. But he leaves behind 115 poems composed while behind bars. He is concerned for them. Out of the 115 he has therefore attempted to copy at least 60.

If this little book comes into your hands, write out a fair copy carefully and accurately, keep it in a safe place and after the war get it to Kazan, have it published as the poems of the Tatar people's dead poet. That is my dying wish.

Musa Jalil. 1943. December

INSCRIPTION ON FRONT COVER OF FIRST NOTEBOOK

December 1943

In prison September 1942-November 1943—wrote 125 verses and one big poem. But will they ever see the light? They'll die with me.

NOTE ON THE MARGIN OF A GERMAN BOOK DISCOVERED BY SOVIET SOLDIERS IN MOABIT PRISON LIBRARY

Not later than March 1944

I, well-known Tatar poet Musa Jalil, am locked in the Moabit gaol for my politics and am sentenced to be shot. . . . Please give my best regards to A. Fadeyev, P. Tychina and my family.

Musa Jalil (Musa Zalilov), the celebrated Tatar poet, was born in 1906 into a poor peasant family in the village of Mustafino, near Orenburg. After joining the Y.C.L. in 1919 he began to write poetry, sounding the call for battle for Soviet power. After finishing his studies he took up full-time Y.C.L. work and wrote poetry at the same time. One of his early works was the libretto to the famous Tatar opera *Altynchech*. In 1939, he was elected President of the Tatar Union of Writers.

At the very outset of the war Musa Jalil joined the army and after taking a political workers' training course he was posted to the Volkhov Front, to the 2nd Strike Force. In July of 1942, he ran into an ambush near Myasnoi Bor and, badly wounded, was taken prisoner and put in a prison camp near Helm in Poland. At the end of the year he was still a sick man when he was transferred to the Demblinski p.o.w. camp where he commenced his illegal work against the nazis. The next spring Jalil was dispatched to Germany, to the Wustrau camp not far from Berlin. On instructions from the underground he began operating in the "Ideal Urals" committee, which recruited legionnaires for Hitler's army among the Tatars, Bashkirs and other Soviet eastern nationalities. Utilising his opportunity of visiting many war camps, Jalil did what he could to see that an underground group was operating well in every camp. Together with Jalil in the resistance organisation was Abdulla Alishev, Tatar children's writer, whom Musa Jalil knew from Kazan, Ahmed Simayev, a Moscow journalist, an old friend of Jalil's from his Zamoskvorechye days when he worked at a Tatar young workers' home, Garif Shabayev, insurance agent from Tashkent, engineer Fuad Bulatov, etc.

213

Musa Jalil (Musa Zalilov), Hero
of the Soviet Union

In early summer 1943, Jalil left for the Tatar legion's Central Edlin camp, situated near Radom, some 70 miles south of Warsaw. The propaganda company in which Jalil worked was made the underground centre in the Edlin camp. The underground fighters were preparing for an uprising. But on the night of August 12, all the underground members were arrested after being given away by a traitor. First they were sent to a Warsaw gaol, then to Berlin, to the Moabit prison. The investigation dragged on for six months until eventually, in March 1944, a Dresden court sentenced them all to the firing squad. After the sentence, Jalil and his companions languished in Berlin's Tegel and Spandau gaols. They were executed at the end of the year.

Musa Zalilov (Jalil) was posthumously awarded the title of Hero of the Soviet Union and his literary works gained the supreme Soviet award—the Lenin Prize.

His friends kept the three notebooks in which he had written his beautiful poems. The first book contains sixty poems in closely-written Arabic ligature. It was presented to the Tatar Union of Writers in 1946. The second book, containing fifty poems written in Tatar with Latin letters, was handed in at the Soviet Consulate in Brussels in 1947. It had been preserved by André Timmermans, a Belgian anti-fascist who had shared the same cell as Jalil in Moabit. Later on another book came to light.

NOTE
LEFT BY RESISTANCE GIRL FROM SLUTSK

1944

Borya, we are to be killed during the night. The rats can sense their end is coming. I told them to their face that we will win. Borya, please excuse me for causing you so much grief. You know we don't always say and do what we like, and I love you so, so much I don't know how to tell you. Borya, right now I'm in your arms and I'm not afraid, let them take me away. Yesterday, when they walloped me very hard, I whispered to myself "Borya, dear" and told them nothing—I don't want them to hear your name. Borya, bye-bye, thanks for everything.

This note was written on a piece of notepaper by a 19-year-old resistance girl from Slutsk. Her name remains unknown.

PAVEL NESMELOV'S LETTER

Dear comrade,

If you find this letter when I'm dead you must know the truth.... I fired off all my bullets and we held our ground till our last bullet. Shot many Germans. Couldn't keep the positions any longer. Now I lay here wounded in the leg. Next to me lies Timofei Stefanishin, wounded and shell-shocked. Yesterday the two of us laid from dawn to sunset in a vegetable patch, near a woodpile, trying not to be noticed. When darkness fell we found a trench. We spent the night there. January 21 is also drawing to a close. Nothing to eat yesterday or today. To rise and enter the house is dangerous. Germans are all around. We don't fancy falling on the mercies of the Germans and being tortured.

It will soon be night. We don't know what's in store. Maybe death.

Please, comrade, write a letter to my father and my family. I have been two and a half years a prisoner in Rumania and, despite my awful mutilation after the camp, I didn't go home when they set me free.... I wrote home and got no reply. My father, mother, wife and two sons are waiting and hoping for my return. Their address is: Mikhail Nesmelov, Galkin Village Soviet, Vetluga District, Gorky Region.

That's about all. I wish you all the best in finishing the war and hope you never have as much bad luck as me.

Good-bye friend!

Pavel M. Nesmelov

21. 1–45

Before the war Pavel Nesmelov was a secondary school history teacher. In the war he was a fearless fighter.

In January 1942, he was badly wounded and taken to the Feodosia hospital. When the nazis took over the town he became a prisoner. Later he was set free by the Soviet Army. Despite his war wounds, he went out to take his revenge on the enemy. In December 1944, he was hit by a mortar shell splinter. But in January 1945, he was once more fighting at the front.

Pavel Nesmelov's life came to a tragic end. He was once more taken prisoner. His captors dealt with him extremely brutally before shooting him.

Pavel Nesmelov's mutilated body was found on January 24, 1945, at a spot west of the village of Nadivenim (on the west bank of the Danube). This was where his last letter was discovered. It was sent with an accompanying letter by Major Goryunov to *Soviet Warrior*, a frontline newspaper. Major Goryunov's letter read:

"Soldiers of the Red Army, Pavel Nesmelov and Timofei Stefanishin were found near a trench. They had been tortured by the Germans. Nesmelov had had his ears, nose, lower lip and fingers of his right hand cut off. Stefanishin had had his right eye poked out and his nose cut off."

VERSES FROM A NOTEPAD
FOUND IN SACHSENHAUSEN

1943 to January 27, 1945

LAST WISH

If ever it comes that I part with life
In this hated foreign land,
In a prison camp ridden with tears and strife,
If I die here young, and with ruthless hands,
The Germans take up my remains
Relieved at last of unheard-of pains,
To burn me and scatter my dust,—
And you, my beloved brothers and friends,
You whom I treasure and trust,
Will not be there to attend my end—
Rise like a man with your militant songs
And fight to revenge our wrongs.
Rise undaunted for your rightful cause,
Smash those walls and fling open those doors,
Lift the red banner of victory
High in the sky for the world to see.
The suffering millions will join your ranks
Like a mighty river that floods its banks.
The struggle will bring its fruits, I know.
Our forces will deal a shattering blow
At the vicious eagle who tears our land.
Revived and mighty again it will stand.
When you draw the account, dear comrades,
Of our sufferings, triumphs, defeats,
Do not be too hard, dear comrades,
On those whom the German so cruelly treats.
Remember the fallen heroes,
Carry their names in your hearts,
Mention them in your victory songs
When the great celebration starts.

* * *

218

I will be with you again, dear Russia.
To admire your rivers' mighty spread,
To listen to the murmur of your forests,
To tread the paths my fathers used to tread.
 Long, long since I sang among your flowers,
 Revelled in the fragrance of your streams,
 And sat beneath the over-hanging oak-boughs
 With the blue-eyed darling of my dreams.
Yet I am with you, with you forever,
For the moment sleep invades my eyes
I dream myself together with my darling
On the path that by the lakeside lies.
 I will be with you again, dear Russia,
 To admire your rivers' mighty spread,
 To listen to the murmur of your forests,
 To tread the paths my fathers used to tread.

* * *

How I wish I could see you today,
And walk in the shadowy park,
For the murmuring Dnieper to listen and smile
At our whispers exchanged in the dark.
 I wish I could press you close to my heart,
 Hold you tenderly in my arms,
 And kiss, and kiss, and kiss without end
 Your face, your shoulders, your palms.
But my dreams are in vain—for you I am dead,
And the love in your heart will die,
And I must follow my thorny path
And remember you with a sigh.

* * *

I cannot forget the land of my birth
Where my childhood and youth I spent.
Full of love is my soul for its sacred soil,
Which these verses of mine give vent.

A love which I bear through all tortures and grief,
In Gestapo's most fearful vaults,
A love that helps me to stand without tears
The murderers' taunts and assaults.

219

I open my soul unashamed in these lines—
He is blameless who meets his lot
Never bowing before the detested foe,
Whether destined to live or not.

* * *

My stubborn heart drives away my fears
And revives the dear old scenes,
Rejecting the thought that I may be shot
Ere the first light of morning gleams.
Reassured, I attend to the voice of my dreams
And I don't know how, but it somehow seems
That until I die I shall see once more
All that I cherished and loved before,
Everything that is now so far;
Hope shines in the joyless gloom like a star.
If only I could live to the day
When victory comes in its wreath of May.
How I want to live—I am still so young!
How I want to be my dear friends among!
But again and again the dark shadow of doubt
Puts the feeble light of my faint hopes out.
And yet, though seized by the anguish of
death,
I am loyal to you to my very last breath,
To you, my Motherland! May you thrive
When I am no longer alive.

A notepad and verses were unearthed in 1958 when the former Sachsenhausen concentration camp was being cleared out. The camp site is quite near Oranienburg, about thirteen miles north of Berlin. The leader of a building team Wilhelm Hermann came across the tattered writing pad amidst the ruins of the camp barracks. It is still possible to make out the words "Unforgettable. Verses in Captivity", written on the yellowed cover. Wilhelm Hermann gave the verses to Senior Lieutenant Molotkov, a Soviet officer serving in one of the Soviet Army units in Germany.

On December 31, 1958, the newspaper *Soviet Army* (for Soviet troops serving in Germany) got news of the find and published five verses. A few days later a report and some poems of the unknown Soviet patriot appeared in *Red Star* and *Komsomolskaya Pravda*. Despite all efforts, it has not yet been possible to establish the identity

The first page of the notepad found in Sachsenhausen

of the poet. It has been suggested, however, that there was more than one author. This appears likely from the fact that the verses are entered into the notebook in even, firm handwriting with few mistakes and no corrections. Many of the verses were known farther abroad than Sachsenhausen; inmates of Ravensbrück, Buchenwald and others claim knowledge of some of the verses. In their letters to editorial office former prisoners suggest such names as Pyotr from Kharkov, Victor from Donetsk, a certain Nikolai, Ivan Kolyuzhny, and some others, as the authors. French Communist Salvador Charlie, to whom one of the poems is dedicated, remembers being friendly with a Russian inmate named Yuri Stolyarov who used to read him his own poetry. Two acrostics in the notebook contain the names of Anton Parkhomenko and Ivan Kolyuzhny. It may be these are the authors of the poems or just the poet's friends.

Former Ravensbrück inmate Zinaida Golubeva, whose poem "A Maiden's Song from Ravensbrück Concentration Camp" appears in the notebook, recounted that during her time in Ravensbrück she corresponded with one of the male prisoners (they tied a note to a stone and threw it over two walls from the men's section of the camp to the women's and back) who signed himself as "Ivan", "Ivan-Star" or "Ivan-Star-Thorn". In reply to her "A Maiden's Song..." he sent her "To the Dead Friend" and other verses. In his last note he mentioned being taken away. That was the last she heard of him; he was probably moved to Sachsenhausen.

The story how the notebook happened to be at the barracks gradually unfolded from the letters that came to newspaper editorial offices. The notebook was found in that part of the barrack ruins which once served as a kitchen in the "Sonderlager". This special camp was constructed between 1943 and 1944 for especially important prisoners, including high-ranking officers of Hitler's Wehrmacht suspected of being implicated in a plot to assassinate the Führer. In 1945, the barracks were repaired by a special gang from the "Sonderlager" which included Germans, Norwegians, Russians and other nationalities. The chief electrician responsible for repairs of the camp electric wires was Martin Gauslo, a Norwegian prisoner. After the war, he wrote to a friend that while wiring an electric circuit in the special camp he was asked by Russian friends to hide a notebook containing some verses in a wall. He wrote:

"Dear friend,

"As I mentioned to you before, I drew up a plan of the kitchen barracks in the special camp and marked the spot where I hid the manuscript containing a collection of poems of a Russian poet in Sachsenhausen. It should be under the floor of the kitchen just in front of the wall I have marked. If you intend to write there you can tear off the plan and attach it to the letter. Very best wishes,

"Martin Gauslo."

As far as he can remember, the notebook was handed to him at the beginning of 1945 by a Russian inmate named Mark Tilevich, who had asked him to hide it—which he had done, wrapping the notebook in a piece of rubberised material.

Mark Tilevich recalls that two members of the electricians' gang used to read the verses jotted down in the notebook—Victor from Donetsk and a doctor, Stepan Gun, who died on V-Day. But Mark Tilevich cannot remember the author of the verses. Quite possible it was Victor, for the name of Victor is mentioned by other former inmates as a poet.

Whoever it was who wrote the verses in the notebook, he was certainly a real Soviet patriot, whose spirit was not broken by any of the humiliation or the whole regime of indignity which the Germans had developed to a fine art. In the nazi concentration camps everything was done to break a person down both physically and morally, to trample on his feelings and destroy everything human in him. Sachsenhausen was the graveyard of inmates from 27 European nations. The camp officers and kapos put to death more than 100,000 prisoners. In 1941 alone, 18,000 Soviet officers and men were brutally exterminated here. On April 21, 1945, about 30,000 survivors of the camp were driven northwards, to the Baltic, where they were to be loaded on barges and sunk. This really was a march of death: thousands of emaciated, exhausted people remained forever by the roadside—a guard would shoot anyone who could not move any farther. Perhaps the owner of the notebook was among these unfortunates from Sachsenhausen.

The author, or authors, whichever the case may be, will long remain an example of heroism, extraordinary bravery and noble feelings.

The notepad of checkered paper contains fifty poems. The verses are written in a small, clear hand, boldly lettered in indelible pencil. The last poem is dated January 27, 1945.

INSCRIPTION
IN JUN. LT. IVAN LANDYSHEV'S Y.C.L. CARD

March 15, 1945

I am not afraid, I feel no weariness in my arms, and I shall fight the foe and be devoted to my country until my last drop of blood!

After completely liberating Soviet territory towards the end of 1944 the Soviet Army battered the enemy on his own land. In March 1945, units of the 2nd Byelorussian Front, together with troops of the 3rd Byelorussian Front who had overrun and pressed back to the

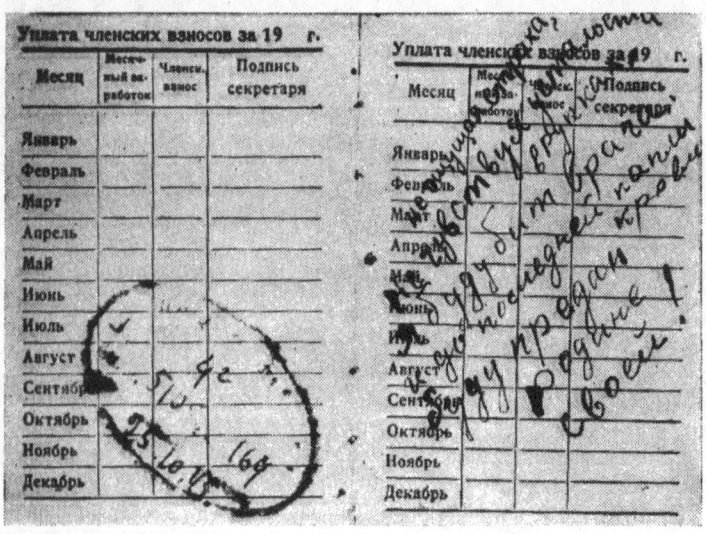

Ivan Landyshev's Y.C.L. card

Ivan Landyshev

sea enemy forces in Eastern Prussia, began to advance into Pomerania. Towards mid-March, the enemy made a last ditch stand at the approaches to Stettin.

Jun. Lt. Landyshev's unit broke through the Germans' first line of defence and a pitched battle commenced in front of the second line of trenches. In the heat of the combat, the company commander fell. Twenty-year-old Ivan Landyshev took over command of the company.

The young officer did not lose his head. After issuing orders, he led a charge. His group of men gained a hold in the enemy dug-outs and hand-to-hand fighting started. During the skirmishing, Ivan Landyshev was seriously wounded. But he continued to direct the fighting. Feeling his strength ebbing away, he took out his Y.C.L. card and scrawled his dying vow on the last page with the blood oozing from his open wounds. Ivan Landyshev died on March 15, 1945. After the battle his comrades buried the hero on Polish soil.

FROM DIARY
OF P.O.W. BORIS NOZDRIN

Vesprem, on Lake Balaton, Hungary
16th March, 1945

... I feel my release from captivity is near at hand. At a time like this I feel like describing the whole of my life, recalling everything. I feel like describing all the terrible things the Germans did to the people they conquered. I feel like describing all my hatred towards the enemy. I feel like describing all my love for Russia, which I feel so keenly at this moment. I can just imagine how lovely life will be after the war, how people will respect one another after these terrible trials of war. People will really value one another. . . .

I have Russia. I belong to her with all my very being, and my life is for her. And over there in Russia lies my homeland —Siberia and the beautiful village of Ushur, and there lives my beloved with the simple Russian name of Masha. There aren't any apples or grapes there, but they do have nuts, all sorts of berries, and we will plant orchards there. Wherever I've been, I have never forgotten Siberia. Her riches, the taiga—golden forests and furry animals, and her fields—a second Ukraine. What a marvellous future ahead of her!

April 1945, Austria

Only half of us left—the rest have all been slaughtered. For two days now we haven't had anything to eat and we work more than all the others. We're working day and night. My strength is running out.

Oh, my native land! If only I could see you as I see you in my dreams. Oh, my native Russia, my invincible homeland. A word of greeting I send you from my dingy prison. In thought I walk about the Siberian expanses, but my strength is running out. . . .

Minsk
    Baranovichi
        Lublin
            Uzhgorod
                Budapest
                    Vesprem
                        Sharvar

That is my hard trail. I'll try to remember everything, all the places, all the indignities, the whole back-breaking trail. And I'll describe it all, everything, if I live I'll write a book *In Captivity*. Right at this moment some thing or other comes back to me. I recall one date. That was January 17 or 18, 1942. I received a bad head wound near the village of Oskui, Leningrad Region, Chudov District. I came to my senses and well remember Minsk, a prisoner-of-war camp. I remember sitting next to a student in horn-rimmed spectacles, Kostya, and an interned soldier—either a Kazakh or a Bashkir—Bisinchakeyev. Then the gates flew open and an old man was pushed in. He staggered forward, his arms flapping, lips trembling, wanting to say something, but apparently unable to do so. Blood trickled down his long, grey beard and on his bald head there was a raw and bloody wound—a five-pointed star had been carved out. He took a few more steps and fell, stretching himself as after waking up, and then died with his eyes open. We ran up. "Professor!" cried Kostya and began to sob. He told me he had been one of his professors.

In Uzhgorod I met a nicely dressed Russian girl—Nina Morozova from Gomel. She begged me to kill her because she was being forced at gun-point to live with a German officer. Instead of killing her I got her to change into soldier's uniform, and she lived with us as a captured soldier. She lived like that for a long time, then one day the guards noticed she was a girl, and a German soldier raped her and slit her throat before our very eyes.

Boris Nozdrin, born 1921, was taken prisoner, as his notes indicate, in January 1942 after being wounded in the head during fighting near the village of Oskui. He saw many war camps. When Soviet troops advanced into Hungary and Austria, the nazis decided to wipe out all Russian prisoners. Nozdrin was shot together with thousands of other Soviet people in early April 1945. His diary was noticed in the pocket of his service jacket as Soviet soldiers were burying the mutilated corpses of their fellow countrymen.

VLADIMIR CHURSIN'S TESTAMENT

April 16, 1945

LAST WISH

I go into battle with complete awareness of the task entrusted me by the Communist Party.

And if I die, please know that I gave my life for my country. I ask my comrades-in-arms not to stop until they see the walls of Berlin.

16/IV—45

Best wishes,
V. I. Chursin

The war was coming to an end. The fighting had switched to the lair of the nazi beast. The day of atonement was drawing near for all the atrocities the nazis had committed in Europe. Hitler's men were putting up a desperate resistance. The Soviet troops were bearing down on the German capital and Hitler's army command had decided to put up a last ditch fight for Berlin. At the approaches to the city and in the city itself, the nazis had set up a strong system of fortifications and concentrated about a million soldiers around the town supported by a large number of artillery and tanks.

The decisive push into Germany took place between April 16 and May 2 by troops of the 1st Ukrainian, 1st and 2nd Byelorussian fronts.

Nineteen-year-old Vladimir Chursin wrote his last wish just before the battle for Berlin. He was killed a little later in the last battle. His comrades buried the courageous youngster and wrote on his Y.C.L. card: "Your comrades have fulfilled your last wish—Berlin is ours."

PAVEL YABLOCHKIN'S LETTER

Not later than April 25, 1945

Mum,

I'm taking a breather. So I have a bit of time to talk to you.

What a pity it has to be our last conversation. It would be wonderful if you never get the letter, but saw me instead.

I'll be writing it and carrying it next to my heart, so that if I'm killed some time or other we'll still be together, you and I, like we were before.

I left you for a time. Don't you cry, Mum! I only want to ask you one thing—to look after my son Alyosha. He'll be without a father. Give him a kind pat on the head, tell him a story and give him a kiss for me.

A year has already gone by since I escaped from the p.o.w. camp. I saw a lot during my six months' inside! They forced us to look. Mum, you just can't imagine, you've no idea. Whenever I think of it ... if only I could find the words to curse them, but words don't suffice. May they be cursed a thousand times by all the people of the world and burn in hell, may they be sent to feed the worms—and even the worms would turn their noses up at them.

Elderly and middle-aged people were carefully spaced out facing each other and buried in the earth up to their waists. A line of tow was spread from one to the other. Paraffin was then poured on and a horrible chorus of heart-rending screams came from amidst the blaze. But those swine were like blocks of wood, like stone idols, grinning and cackling.

Mum,

I've seen them take little children like Alec, tear them from their mothers' hands, grab hold of them by the legs, give them a swing and hurl them down a well.

I've never been a believer in God, you know that, Mum. Yet at times like that I've prayed to the Almighty, begged with all my soul, that my nerves would stand the strain. Many of us couldn't hold out, fainted or rushed to intervene—they were shot in the legs and had their clothes lashed off of them on the spot. Then salted like meat, and watered methodically until they came to, sprinkled with salt again ... then the Germans, going mad like wild beasts, chopped them into bits.

After all their fiendish tricks, the bastards are now taking to their heels. Now they're scared of us like the plague. But the truth will catch up with them and ferret them out wherever they are. We'll give them a fair trial. After the war the stern people of the whole world will see that they get their deserts for the endless suffering and torments they caused.

Don't you cry, now. I didn't die, just went away from you, Mum, like many went away, the same sort of people as me. We went away fighting for our people, wiping barbarity and slavery off the face of the earth. Went away for a happy future for all people of the world as well as our own.

Mum, the war will be over, the country will heal its deep wounds and once again people will begin to live in freedom. Before you know it my Alec will be finishing school and learning a trade of a locomotive driver.

No one would dare to be so inhuman or shameless as to help again let loose any monsters like there are today. The whole world would never let the Huns set the earth alight a second time.

Build, live, work, study, and if you want to do us an honour then band together and mop up the enemy quickly and get over your war wounds, create a happy life for everyone. . . .

Good-bye, Alec and Mum. Lots of kisses to you both.

I've been sitting up too late. Off for a kip. My comrades—a great bunch of fighters—are asleep.

Your Pavel Yablochkin

Pavel Yablochkin was formerly a farmer from Yakshino on the Volga. In the early part of the war he was captured, escaped and was soon back with a rifle in his hands fighting the enemy. In fact, he was several times cited for bravery. He was killed in Eastern Prussia in the spring of 1945. This letter, soaked with the blood of her son, was delivered to his mother.

LETTER HOME
SENT BY SEN. LT. DOLGOV,
COMMANDING OFFICER OF A TANK COMPANY

Not later than May 2, 1945

Mum,

You are probably completely worn out. You must have a load of worries, my dear. It's hard to imagine how you get by with all that crowd to look after.

Mum, please don't worry yourself over me. Everything is just grand. A soldier's duty is quite simple—we get on with the battle. We're trying to finish off the nazis as quickly as we can. When the war is over and we're all together again, I'll tell you a lot about myself—how I lived, how we fought.

You keep writing to tell me to watch out for myself a bit more. Please excuse me, Mum, but that's impossible. I'm a commanding officer. Who's going to show the men an example if their commanding officer starts thinking of trying to save his skin rather than winning the battle. Please understand, Mother, that I cannot do this although, of course, I'd very much like to get through this war and stay alive so as I can come back again to my home town and meet all of you.

All my love,
Sasha

Alexander Dolgov was born in 1917 in the village of Bolshoye Tomilovo, near Kuibyshev.

Thirteen years later he began work on the local collective farm and a little later left for one of the big factories in Chapayevsk, where his brothers worked. Together with other factory hands, he was called up in 1938.

Alexander Dolgov, Hero of the
Soviet Union

Ten months later, when the Japanese troops invaded the Mongolian People's Republic near the river Khalkhin-Gol, Private Dolgov was in one of the units sent to beat off the Japanese attacks.

In August 1939, the Japanese invaders were finally repelled. On the recommendation of his superiors, Private Dolgov was sent to a regimental school which he finished with honours. Soon afterwards the Germans attacked and he left for four years at the front.

The tank unit of the 1st Byelorussian Front in which Sen. Lt. Dolgov's tank company served, had the enemy on the run back to Berlin. Towards the war's end, Dolgov was given the responsible task of piercing the enemy's defence at one particularly stubborn point of the fighting. He gathered his tank men around him, explained the situation and called on them to keep up the good name of the Guards in combat. As always, the commanding officer's tank was first into the attack. By his skill and fearlessness he was a great inspiration to his men and the Soviet tanks soon ripped through the enemy's defence and pushed on into Berlin. The way ahead through the central defence sector was open.

In the morning of April 30, fighting flared up again for the centre of the German capital. By the afternoon, at precisely 2.25 p.m. Soviet troops had captured the Reichstag and run up the Victory flag. The Berlin garrison laid down their arms and were taken prisoner.

Berlin had fallen. For the third time in history Russian soldiers victoriously passed through the Brandenburg Gates.

Together with other front units, Sen. Lt. Dolgov's tank company moved on farther, to the city of Brandenburg, some 40 miles west of Berlin. The tank company commander's actions were referred back to H.Q. for commendation.

Alexander Dolgov led his tanks with just as much daring and battlecraft onto Brandenburg. But he was not to see the V-Day—a German shell blew up his tank in the very last battle.

By decree of the Supreme Soviet of the U.S.S.R. Alexander Dolgov was posthumously awarded the title of Hero of the Soviet Union.